PUBLIC AND PROFESSIONAL SPEAKING

PUBLIC AND
PROFESSIONAL SPEAKING

A Confident Approach for Women

Barbara Berckhan, Carola Krause
and Ulrike Roeder

Translated by Arabella Spencer

'an association in which the free development of each
is the condition of the free development of all'

FREE ASSOCIATION BOOKS / LONDON / NEW YORK

First published in the United Kingdom 2000 by
FREE ASSOCIATION BOOKS
57 Warren Street, London W1P 5PA

Translation © 2000 Arabella Spencer

Originally published in German as:
Die erfolgreichere Art (auch Männer) zu überzeugen
© 1999 Kösel-Verlag GmbH & Co., Munich

The right of the contributors to be identified as the authors
of this work has been asserted by them in accordance with the
Copyright, Designs and Patents Act 1988

A CIP record for this book is available from the British Library

ISBN 1 85343 473 6 pbk

Designed and produced for the publisher by
Chase Production Services, Chadlington, OX7 3LN
Printed in the European Union by J.W. Arrowsmith, Bristol

Contents

Preface

Under a surface of fear lies your power of persuasion. It is trapped down there. For as long as the fear of speaking imprisons you, your personality will not be able to develop to the full. If your fear abated, your power of persuasion would again come to light. You would no longer have to be restricted by a fear of speaking.

This book presents tried and tested methods with which you can break down your fear. We show you techniques that go right to the root cause and bring about a change at that level. In the process you will learn to recognise your speech inhibitions more easily and discover a lot about how they are strengthened or made less severe. Fear can be reduced step by step. And in exactly the same way you can build up your speaking abilities step by step. In this book we offer you numerous tips and methods with which you can develop your own style of speaking.

It has been very carefully set out: to begin with it deals with the issue of understanding your fear or inhibitions and of getting to know them better. Subsequently you will be shown how you can reduce your fear of speaking. If you can speak more freely and casually in front of other people, your style of speaking will become more important. Whoever has suffered from fear and inhibitions for a long time has avoided many situations that necessitate speaking. And so you may simply have had little opportunity in the course of time to practice. Anxious people often lack experience and practice. But you need rhetorical strength in order to get your message across successfully. You can easily acquire these speaking abilities with the aid of our tips and techniques. And at the end of our book we demonstrate how you can develop persuasive arguments. But to begin with there is the issue of breaking free from the cage of fear. When you have left this prison behind you it will be easy to start winning people over to your way of thinking.

1 The Fear of Speaking: A Fear with Many Faces

The fear of speaking is the fear of voicing opinions in front of others, of asking questions, or of giving a speech. There are many situations in which this fear may arise:

- In private circles, at family gatherings and in discussions amongst friends
- At meetings, in club situations, at action groups or parent evenings
- In professional situations, at conferences or staff meetings
- At school, college or university
- Public appearances on television, in lecture theatres or on the stage

The fear of speaking, which may also be described as the fear of speaking in public, the fear of an audience, speech inhibition or stage fright, is one of the most common fears. Many people know what it is like to feel nervous when they are expected to speak in public. A representative survey conducted in the US revealed that over 40 per cent of people were scared of speaking in group situations. From our seminars we know that the fear of speaking manifests itself to varying degrees, from slight nervousness to strong agitation all the way through to downright panic. This not only varies from person to person, but is dependent on the situation in which a person is expected to speak. For most people it is true that the more important the occasion for speaking is, that is to say, the more important the evaluation of what they have to say is – as is the case, for example, in examinations – the greater the fear. Another factor determining the degree of fear is the size of the audience: many people are less scared of speaking in front of a handful of people than in front of a crowd of a thousand listeners. Similarly, the relationship with the audience plays a role: the more familiar, informal and close the people are, the less scary the situation proves to be. On the other hand, most people find it more difficult to speak in front of strangers, superiors, people in authority or people upon whose judgement they depend. Taking a closer look at what is actually said reveals the extent to which degrees of fear vary. Some people report that they find it easy to talk about personal matters, but that they run into trouble where they have to speak in professional situations, about things that, so to speak, have 'rhyme and reason'. Some people, on the other hand, find themselves on safe ground when they are required to give professional speeches – 'I know what I am talking about' – but find that they are very scared when it comes to speaking about anything personal or emotional.

Irrespective of the situation in which there is a requirement to speak, there is one common factor: the fear of speaking is a form of social fear, that is, the fear of other people, and behind the term 'fear of speaking' there in fact lies a whole host of possible fears that may all be described as social fears:

- Fear of rejection
- Fear of criticism
- Fear of failure
- Fear of success
- Fear of being alone
- Fear of closeness
- Fear of being the centre of attention
- Fear of making mistakes
- Fear of authority etc.

Collectively all these fears amount to the fear of being judged by other people. It is one of the nightmare scenarios of most people who are scared of speaking in public to lose face in front of an audience, to be hissed or booed at, laughed at or criticised. Most people who say they are scared of speaking in public know the feeling of constantly assessing themselves and being on the lookout for how they are assessed by others. In technical terminology this is called 'heightened public self-awareness'; this means that when in contact with other people, individuals place particular importance on what other people think of them. This leads to their directing much of their own attention on themselves. For example, they may ask themselves 'How do I look?' or 'Do they think what I'm saying is stupid?' or 'Why is that guy over there smirking like that? Is he smirking at me?' People like this feel that they are under constant scrutiny and have developed highly sensitive antennae to their surroundings; they gauge other people's reactions according to an inner rubric: 'Am I coming across or not? Am I doing well? Have I failed?' and so on. It goes without saying that this 'heightened public self-awareness' inevitably has a negative effect on the way the people who suffer from it speak. Speaking is in itself a highly complex process: We think, search for the right words to express our thoughts, say them whilst simultaneously thinking ahead to make the logical connection, take a breath, add spontaneous ideas or incorporate questions from the audience and so on. If at the same time we are trying to look at ourselves from an objective point of view, are listening to what we are saying and are trying to assess ourselves through the eyes of the public, the chances of losing the thread or beginning to stumble over our words may increase. The very fear of somehow speaking wrongly provokes precisely that which is feared.

Just what is it that so many people find threatening about situations in which they have to speak? Firstly they fear the negative consequences of saying the wrong thing, for example the consequences of a messed-up exam or of an interview that goes horribly wrong. But most situations in which people are expected to say something do not involve life-changing or life-threatening dangers. Nevertheless, many people experience fear even in these situations. What they are scared of is the possibility of their own weaknesses and inadequacies coming to light, or of others rejecting them for what or who they are. What is under threat is their own self-esteem, something that can be shaken by the assessment of others.

Is it only women who experience the fear of speaking? No. This fear spans the sexes. Men too suffer from this fear. And yet it is not without reason that we have written this book for women:

Women's fear of speaking in public is particularly obstinate, it seems more normal for women because it fits so well with their traditional role. The public is traditionally a man's realm, women are assigned to privacy, to home and family: Women listen and understand, men speak. This classic image is particularly poignant for women who wish to speak in public. On the whole, women are less confident. They receive less attention, are interrupted more frequently and back down from the positions they adopt more quickly than men. In general, women more readily admit their fears, because fear corresponds to the social expectations of women. There is a string of men who display obvious fear when speaking but cannot admit this to themselves or to others. We will outline in detail in a later chapter how well the fear of speaking in public seems to go hand in hand with being a woman. Moreover, we will also go into the 'more poignant conditions' with which women, unlike men, are confronted in situations where they are required to speak. This book is intended to support women who wish to understand and overcome their fears.

How Does the Fear of Speaking Manifest Itself?

The fear of speaking can be felt or become evident in various ways. From the experience of our seminars we know how variously women experience their fear. Some are already agitated days before they are due to speak in front of people and have sleepless nights, whereas others appear completely cool and laid back when speaking in public, but subsequently feel as if they have just spoken under anaesthetic and no longer remember anything. Others are practiced speakers who shake like a leaf after having given a talk and criticise themselves mercilessly. Many are so agitated that they deal with the situation by just ceasing to speak.

The fear of speaking in public not only affects the body, but also thought processes and behaviour. Let us look at these three levels more closely. You will probably recognise your own symptoms somewhere in the following.

The Effects on the Body

The body usually offers up a distinct reaction to fear: If a person considers a situation to be dangerous or threatening, information relating to the threat is passed on via the autonomic nervous system to the adrenal glands, which instantly release two stress hormones, adrenaline and noradrenaline. These are distributed around the body via the bloodstream and trigger a survival reaction in the body. In life-threatening situations these offer the body the first possibility of attacking or retreating. The body immediately starts to perform at its maximum; the thought process is temporarily blocked since protracted thought would be an impediment in a dangerous situation. Instead, cardiac activity and metabolism are increased, the whole body is prepared for a confrontation with danger. These physical changes, which are produced by the release of hormones, are the physical cause of all the unpleasant sensations that can prove to be such an obstacle in situations in which you are required to speak: Your heart beats faster, your hands become clammy, your knees begin to shake, your face becomes pale or red, or the mental block mentioned above takes place, your head is empty. This is what is called a 'blackout'.

The Effects on Thought Processes

Fear impedes creative thought. A blackout is an extreme example of this. But even at the stage of preparing a speech, we may find that nothing more comes to mind, that it is difficult to concentrate, or that we cannot remember anything. Frequently our thoughts go round in circles, and mostly they revolve around the dreaded situation rather than the contents of our speech, for example: 'I hope nothing goes wrong', 'It would be awful if ...', 'God, I mustn't ...' It is precisely these thoughts that increase our fear – later we shall consider this in greater detail.

The Effects on Behaviour

Fear can also be identified from the way we behave. Frequently it makes us become fidgety, frantic and tense. Often our gestures become inappropriate or exaggerated, or we appear stiff and frozen. Fear often has us digging our nails into a table or manuscript, or it makes us become restless or has us jiggle a foot. We start speaking unusually quickly or long-windedly, without any pauses, even for breath. Our sentences become confused or we lose the thread altogether – you can probably complete this list from your own experience.

In listing these factors it becomes clear how many symptoms of fear there are that can impede speech and how easily this can result in the fear of fear itself. With this, it is the fear symptoms themselves that generate fear ('I just hope I don't get scared otherwise I'll get all mixed up!'), and many people prefer to avoid or draw back from situations where they are required to speak, thereby sidestepping the need to experience this fear. But this evasive behaviour merely serves to reinforce the fear, it does nothing to resolve it (see Chapter 3). At the same time, because of this evasion we decrease the space we have in which to live our lives and unnecessarily limit ourselves in terms of our personal development and possibilities of experience.

2 Understanding the Fear of Speaking: Causes and Effects

Now that we have outlined what the fear of speaking is and have had an initial glance at the symptoms that accompany it, it is time to consider the cause of this fear. The fear of speaking, along with other fears, originates in our heads, amongst our thoughts. More precisely: fear arises from the thoughts with which we tell ourselves what to do. We dictate to ourselves that we must be a particular way or that something in particular must not be allowed to happen. Such thoughts, with which we give ourselves instructions, run along the lines of: 'Oh God! I mustn't blush now' or 'I must make sure that I don't lose the thread whilst speaking.'

These instructions directed at ourselves are also called imperatives. They are thoughts with which we make rules for ourselves. They are the central cause of our fear when speaking in public. Such internal rules may also be the cause of other strong feelings, for example of anger, despair or depression. We will confine ourselves here to the connection between these orders and the fear of speaking. For the word imperative we also use such terms as 'inner rules' or 'orders given to ourselves'. In this book we will show you how to recognise and dismantle your inner rules. It is important therefore that we begin with a discussion of the background of this issue, thereby making it clearer why we give ourselves instructions and how the fear of speaking arises as a result of the orders that we direct at ourselves.

INNER RULES

If you are thinking about an approaching situation in which you will have to speak and you have thoughts such as 'I mustn't make a fool of myself!', 'I must be persuasive!', 'I should only speak if I am one hundred per cent sure about what it is that I am speaking about!' you are making rules for yourself. All these sentences, irrespective of whether they are thought on an inner level or spoken out loud, typify the orders that we give ourselves. You can identify your own rules most clearly from the phrases that express coercion, such as:

'I must ...!'
'I should ...!'
'I must not ...!'
'The others should ... and may not ...!'

(In the third chapter in the section 'On the way to Feeling more at Ease: Confronting Fear' we will show you other linguistic features of inner rules.)

Even if the rule is directed at how others should behave or what others are not allowed to do, we are still dealing with an order that we have directed at ourself. If I lay down the rule for myself: 'The audience must like me!' or 'The listeners must not reject me!', then I am not seriously trying to dictate to the listeners that they must like me. On the contrary, I am trying to banish from my personal reality the possibility of my being rejected by the audience. It is not allowed to happen that the audience rejects me! If it did happen it would be awful for me, and that is why it must not happen under any circumstances.

How We Push Away What Is Not Allowed to Be

An order directed at ourself represents the attempt to push away or ignore what would be awful or bad for us. Let us assume that I make myself the rule: 'If I am speaking, I must not lose the thread or go off at a tangent.' If it were in actual fact impossible for me to lose the thread whilst speaking or go off at a tangent, I would be on safe ground. I would not be able to violate this rule and would therefore not need to formulate it. But I do make rules for myself because the possibility does in actual fact exist that things could turn out differently: It could be that I lose the thread. I am conscious of this possibility and I feel uncomfortable when thinking about it. In order not to have to continue experiencing these feelings I try to push them away by giving myself the order 'I must not lose the thread whilst speaking.' This inner rule does nothing to change the fact that I could lose the thread. Forgetting where I was or not knowing how to continue when making a comment or speaking at length can happen. I cannot one hundred per cent guarantee the prevention of this possibility. It can happen to me that I get stuck during my speech – however many internal rules I make to see that this does not happen. The possibility of losing the thread remains in my thoughts. And if I think for a moment about what could happen to me whilst speaking, then the possibility of getting stuck also occurs to me. This notion triggers unpleasant feelings in me which I in turn try to combat with the rule 'I must not lose the thread whilst speaking.' Nevertheless the possibility remains that I might lose the thread. You can already see the circularity of these thoughts.

A vicious circle of thoughts looks something like this:

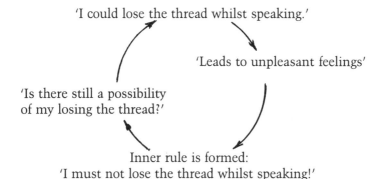

'I could lose the thread whilst speaking.'

'Leads to unpleasant feelings'

'Is there still a possibility
of my losing the thread?'

Inner rule is formed:
'I must not lose the thread whilst speaking!'

This formulating of rules for ourselves may apply to various aspects of our lives and selves:

- to our own physical reaction ('I must not blush!')
- to our own behaviour ('I must speak freely and fluently!')
- to our effect on others ('I must come across as self-assured!')
- to the event ('Nothing is allowed to go wrong!')
- to the reaction of other people ('Others must acknowledge me!')

Similarly, our inner rules may refer to different periods of time. That is to say:

- the future ('I must make a good impression tomorrow!')
- the present ('I mustn't get tense now!')
- the past ('I should have spoken more convincingly yesterday')

Instructions we give ourselves can also just be brief inner directives, with which we spur ourselves on or pep ourselves up, for example 'Pull yourself together!' or 'Stop stumbling over your words!' We give ourselves these orders to get ourselves going. An example of this is a short wake-up command in the morning, 'Come on now – get out of bed!' followed by the spur to hurry up with 'Get a move on!' This way of forcing – or forbidding – ourselves to do something may at first seem harmless and maybe even completely natural. But with every rule we make for ourselves we put ourselves under pressure and introduce unnecessary stress into our everyday affairs.

The Effects of Inner Rules

When we explain these inner rules in our seminars many women discover just how often it is that they give themselves orders on an inner level. Some women even have the impression that their whole existence constitutes a set of rules. This raises the question of whether we might in fact require these orders to control our behaviour and 'pull ourselves together'.

The short answer is that we do not. We can just as easily give our behaviour a direction without rules. We can think of our intentions as goals, desires, norms or values and realise them. I can wish that my speech runs smoothly and can prepare myself in a way that minimises the possibility of my losing the thread. This constitutes my setting a goal. I can however also dictate to myself my goals and intentions. In doing so I am putting on a kind of strait-jacket. Then I tell myself: 'The speech must run smoothly! I forbid myself lose the thread!' In the making of rules for ourselves lies the inner compulsion that it must be so and not any other way. If I do not attain a goal, it may be unpleasant for me. Behind a rule, however, lies a huge 'bad feeling', an image of catastrophe. It would be 'bad', 'awful' or 'frightful' if what is supposed to happen does not happen. What we call the bad feeling is here a very oppressive feeling, one that consists of:

- the spectre of catastrophe ('If I lose the thread the listeners will snigger at me and nobody will respect me any more.')
- previous psychological damage (being laughed at by the whole class at school) and
- old experiences of powerlessness and helplessness (being humiliated and made a fool of, not being able to defend oneself, with nobody there to support you).

All these damaging experiences and terrifying fantasies congeal on an inner level into a type of emotional clot that we experience as something 'bad' or 'awful'. It is the unpleasant feeling that flares up at the thought of what it is like to stand in front of an audience and make mistakes or make a fool of oneself.

This diffuse bad feeling escapes rational reflection. Most people who suffer from fear of speaking know very well that making a mistake whilst speaking is not really a catastrophe for them. But this realisation does nothing to change the fact that they still see it as 'awful'. And it is precisely this experience of the awful, together with the catastrophe fantasies, old psychological scars and other painful experiences associated with it that we are blocking with the help of orders directed at ourselves. We set an inner must or must-not against the bad feeling that flares up inside us.

Let us at this point summarise the effects that inner rules have on us:

Bodily effects

By giving ourselves rules we put ourselves under pressure. When we make a rule for ourselves we are creating 'steam' on an inner level. This causes particular muscle groups to tense up and the heart rate to speed up, we may experience stomach ache, and our face turns pale or red.

Effects on thoughts

Thought processes are controlled by the inner rules. The respective must or must-not becomes the central thought. Thoughts run around in circles. Creativity and the ability to solve problems are reduced.

Emotional effects

When issuing directives to ourselves there initially arises a feeling of urgency and of duress. If we carry on issuing directives these feelings become more vehement. They cause nervousness, trepidation and fear.

Effects on the ability to perceive

Perception is restricted. We screen out anything that does not relate to what must be or what must not happen. A kind of tunnel vision arises whereby the inner rule acts as a sort of perceptive filter, a filter which only lets through anything to do with the inner order.

Effects on behaviour

Actions become more frantic, distracted or nervous. Posture can become stiffer and more tense or also more expansive. The voice becomes subdued and often begins to sound monotonous or to crack. The rate of speech becomes faster or much slower than usual.

One Inner Rule Chases the Next

So far – for the sake of simplicity – we have shown with the examples that we have given how individual inner rules give rise to the fear of speaking. But from our seminars we know that somebody who is afraid of speaking in front of an audience almost always sets off a series of inner rules. The rules are layered one on top of the other.

Some of these rules are pretty much on the surface, others lie deeper. So for example the rule, 'My voice must not tremble!' may be pretty obvious, pretty near the surface, when it comes to delivering a speech in front of an audience. If you delve a little deeper though, other instructions directed at the self may become apparent, like 'I must give the impression of being confident' or 'I mustn't mess up!'

Typically these layers of rules start with the physical symptoms of fear, for example 'My hands must not shake!' We unearth a deeper level of rules if we ask the question: 'Why would it be bad if my hands were to shake?' The answer usually corresponds to behaviour and could go something like 'If my hands begin to shake …

… I can't speak calmly any more
… I start to get into a muddle
… I lose the thread and so on
… *and that would be terrible!*'

If we at this point also ask a further question: 'Why would it be so bad, for example, to lose the thread?', then the next level of deeper-seated rules is revealed:

'If I lose the thread …
… I will appear incompetent
… it will mean that I'm not concentrating
… I will not be able to continue speaking
… *and that would be terrible!*'

Here too we expose the underlying rule connected with the idea of something terrible and in the process slowly reveal a whole system of prohibitions and rules that are interconnected, including feelings of solitude and premonitions of death.

I've got to say something but I mustn't get a lump in my throat or I won't be able to speak fluently and then I will seem incompetent and then there's a possibility that I won't be taken seriously and then what I have to say will be of no consequence, and then the fact that I am present at all will be irrelevant. (Said in a consultation.)

With the aid of the following chart we would like to shed light on this layering of rules, their super- and subordination. It begins at the top on the first hierarchical level with directives that control body-reactions and ends on the lowest level with existential rules.

One rule chases the next – the levels of rules

	I must …	I must not…
Levels of body reaction	control my body, hold my fear in check.	blush, shake, get clammy hands, get a lump in my throat, let my heart race.
Levels of behaviour	say something, speak fluently, continue the conversation, speak confidently, speak clearly, speak loudly.	stumble over my words, make mistakes, lose the thread, pause too often, speak too quickly/slowly, suddenly laugh or cry, flip out, be boring, get in a fluster,
Levels of self-perception	make a good impression, be witty, be objective, be focused, be competent, be confident, be something special, be important.	spread myself too thinly, be insecure, be silly, be stupid, be superficial, get on people's nerves, reveal too much of myself, be unobjective, be weak, be arrogant, praise myself, be too emotional.
Levels of social contact	be seen, justify the expectations of others, impress others, be superior, be respected, be liked, be noticed, be loved.	be criticised, disappoint, be the centre of attention, be laughed at, be ignored, be judged, be an outsider.
Existential levels	For otherwise I will be alone, of no value, an outcast … (etc.) and my life and my existence will lose all meaning → fantasies + fear of death and: that must not happen!	

As you can see, inner rules can be combined in such a way that one rule drags the next one along after it. When one is activated then the deeper-seated rules are also touched upon and brought into play. In this way the rule 'I must not blush!' may activate commands that refer to being rejected or to total failure.

Speech Knots

Particularly when it comes to women's fear of speaking in public, two contradictory rules often oppose each other, as for example, 'I must make sure I get my say – but I must not go charging in.' Both rules operate at the same level, but they stand in opposition to each another. Most of the time women experience this tangle of rules as an on-the-one-hand/on-the-other-hand conflict.

On the one hand I would like what I do to be appreciated or at least to catch the listeners' attention or be of interest to them. On the other hand I must not show off, must not allow any form of 'I am the greatest' or 'I am great at this.'

These words spoken by one of our clients expresses what many women often experience when speaking in public: two inner rules that oppose each other as if on an inner seesaw. The need to be taken seriously often becomes the opponent of the fear of directing too much attention towards oneself and of being devalued as a woman. Consequently these tricky 'speech knots' often express a side of us that wants to shine and another side that must not be too public, as in the following examples:

I must assert myself! <—> I must not rub anyone up the wrong way!

I must get noticed! <—> I must not be the centre of attention!

I must be perfect! <—> I must not show my perfection!

I must stand out! <—> I must conform and fit in!

If a woman is caught in this kind of inner speech knot then no matter how she behaves she is very likely to violate one side of her rules. If she tries by not speaking at all or by being reticent to escape from a situation in which she is expected to speak, she violates her rule of 'I must show what I am capable of' – one of the rules with which she spurs herself on. If she, on the other hand, becomes active and takes the floor, then she violates her rule of restraint – 'I must not draw too much attention to myself.' The person concerned usually experiences each of her modes of conduct – irrespective of whether she is being active or practising restraint – as inadequate and defective.

Composure Comes from Letting Things Take Their Course

We need inner rules because we do not want to experience painful bad feelings and thoughts. But, as we have seen, these rules land us in a real mess. Through them we put ourselves under pressure and experience stress and fear. We can refrain from ordering ourselves on an inner level to do things if we are prepared to experience what we have up until now pushed away: the bad feeling and fantasies of catastrophe. This is often easier said than done. In our everyday dealings we are used to pushing away what disturbs us and is a nuisance, cutting it off it or eliminating it from our minds. An enthusiastic 'Pull yourself together!' often seems very plausible when trying to overcome difficult situations. We usually have little practice of just letting things be and accepting ourselves. It is more natural for us to want to rid ourselves of feelings that bother us than just let them be as they are, an expression of our unique personality. Furthermore, especially in the case of unpleasant feelings, many people believe that they will never be anything but painful. Our feelings are indeed in motion. If they are not blocked out they tend to grow in intensity, reach a climax, subsequently ease and then die away. This also applies to pleasant feelings, like for example happiness, as well as to unpleasant ones. As a rule we find it easy to accept agreeable feelings and let them arise. However, we generally want to rid ourselves of unpleasant ones by pushing them away and putting an inner rule in front of them. This, however, is a guaranteed way of maintaining and conserving these feelings rather than eliminating them.

Once we have dismantled our inner rules we are no longer trapped in circular thought processes and no longer suffer from tunnel vision. We can experience the reality within and surrounding us as it is. We call this kind of awareness accepting awareness. This at first sounds more complicated than it is. You know this type of accepting awareness from day-to-day experience. If you experience something pleasant, then you perceive it as it is and with all your senses, without pushing it away from you or running away from it.

If, for example, you experience a sunset at sea then you will probably be fully aware of the experience. You watch the red sun slowly sinking on the horizon and see how the light reflects off the water. You feel the air cooling down and hear the roar of the waves. You become conscious of the thoughts and feelings that arise within you. You accept what is happening both within and outside you. You perceive everything as it is. The opposite of this would be to give yourself directives, to formulate rules.

A speech in front of an audience is, however, not a sunset by the sea. When speaking, what is important is your own performance, your own self and your evaluation by others. Accepting perception involves your accepting your feelings and thoughts as they are without wanting to banish anything with a rule. If you perceive a situation in which you will have to speak with an attitude of acceptance, then you will confront the possibility that you may make mistakes whilst speaking, that you may not achieve everything you've set out to achieve. With these thoughts perhaps even 'bad' feelings arise. Not to prescribe oneself anything means being conscious of these feelings and thoughts – without getting worked up or running away from them.

IN THE CENTRE OF FEAR

Until now we have approached the fear of speaking from a theoretical perspective. Let us now consider it from the point of view of those stricken with it. How does the fear of speaking manifest itself in everyday situations? And what is it exactly that women fear?

In our training and advisory sessions we have discovered that there are particular horror scenarios that most people who suffer from fear of speaking dread. These include in particular the fear of:

– being the centre of attention
– blushing
– saying something stupid or incorrect and making a
  complete fool of oneself
– loosing the thread and experiencing a 'blackout'
– being jeered at, rejected or even 'torn to pieces'

Perhaps you will recognise the core of your own fear in some of the following examples.

Being the Centre of Attention

Being the centre of attention is for some people more than just unpleasant. Women who become the centre of attention whilst speaking often feel as if the listeners can see right through them or as if they are being condemned by the looks of their listeners.

> To begin with I was completely calm, but when I stood behind the microphone and everybody could see me I became panicky. I felt completely exposed and unprotected. I thought that the others would see all my weaknesses – my figure, clothing and everything. Suddenly the whole situation became immensely embarrassing. I just wanted the ground to swallow me up.

This is how a 36-year-old administrative employee described her first experience of speaking in front of a larger audience.

The tendency to stay in the background and be modest is connected to rules that many women internalised when they were small girls. So it is not surprising that many women are worried about being considered show-offs if they take the limelight. They are scared of being exposed as impostors.

And because women frequently determine their sense of self-worth via their outer appearance, their own imperfect appearance increases the fear. A crooked nose, messy hair and too many wrinkles become flaws that take on disproportionate importance for the person in question, and at the same time she will block from her mind her attractive sides. In her eyes, the audience turns into an unforgiving censor, ready to find fault everywhere. In reality the speaker cannot know what is going on in the heads of the listeners, whether she is being written off by some members of the audience or whether the majority sympathises with her. She suspects that her own self-criticism and self-devaluation is in the eyes and ears of the listeners. She thinks that the others will judge her with the same severity with which she judges herself: 'Isn't that guy over there smirking because I'm making such a fool of myself?! And the woman in the first row, she's now yawned for the third time ...' And of course this is not because the woman has not slept enough or is suffering in the stale air, but can only be, as far as the speaker is concerned, for the sole reason that her speech is boring.

In most cases the fear of being the centre of attention leads to the affected person's attempting to take in as little as possible of her attention-attracting situation and directing all her attention towards making a quick getaway. In other words, she tries to rattle off what she has to say as quickly as possible using the maxim 'hold you breath and just get through'. In practice this 'hold your breath and just get through' typically looks like this: the speaker who is scared of being the centre of attention tries to take as little notice as possible of the listeners and the attention that they are giving her. She does not look at the audience before commencing her speech, but looks at her manuscript on the speaker's desk or looks up at the ceiling. Whilst quickly rattling off her text, trying not to pause too often, she continues to avoid eye contact with the audience. If she does happen to look up at the circle of listeners she becomes aware that all eyes are on her. She really is the centre of attention. The moment she becomes conscious of this her fear increases. This gives rise to mistakes, pauses, her losing the thread or other interruptions to the flow of her words. In order no longer to remain the centre of attention, the speaker usually brings her speech to a close as quickly as possible. Often she does not take enough time to consider whether she has actually said what she intended to say. She does not make a calm, collected and impressive exit. The speech is more or less broken off abruptly; the sudden end is often marked with the words 'That was it'. Her final words have barely died away and she is already rushing from the podium. With a deep sigh of relief she takes her seat, safe in the knowledge that the attention of the audience can no longer reach her.

The first step towards dismantling this fear of being the centre of attention entails coming face to face with the root of the fear and not trying to avoid it. For this we use an exercise in our training sessions which involves the participants consciously experiencing the situation of being the centre of attention. The woman in question sits (or stands) in front of the group. All the other women are seated in a semicircle in front of her, looking at her. For the woman standing in front of the group this is all about standing in silence in the centre of attention of the others. This puts an end to running away, evasion and a hurried escape. The participant is now sitting or standing in a position from which she would usually want to make a quick getaway: she is the centre of attention of the audience. Here she has time consciously to experience the thoughts and feelings connected with her fear. She is able to discern what is going on around and inside her: she can see the audience sitting there, can hear the noises in the room and note the feelings and thoughts that arise in her. She is required to do nothing other than remain where she is. She will notice that by remaining where she is the unpleasant feeling changes. She perceives how the inner waves of feeling rise and eventually fall, until she feels free to start speaking. In Chapter 3 you can find this exercise in a slightly modified form with the name 'Served up on a Plate'.

'Help, I'm Blushing!'

Many women are afraid of blushing when they are the centre of attention. They want to give an impression of being calm, composed and superior, so that nobody will be able to detect their nervousness. But their red face is a give-away.

As far as turning red is concerned, there is often a great discrepancy between what the individual suspects or feels internally and what is apparent to other people. There are women who turn red in the face and whose increasing redness is noticeable. On the other hand, some feel a kind of hot flush in the face which is not outwardly visible.

The degree of redness is also sometimes overestimated. Many suffer from the false belief that turning red is like an advertisement that flickers through the entire room. In reality the redness is usually minimal, with the listeners hardly even noticing it because they are occupied with what is being said rather than the changes in the skin colour of the speaker.

Blushing is a bodily reaction that happens of its own accord and is very difficult to control at will. When we blush the small blood vessels in the skin expand and the flow of the blood to the head region increases. This can be triggered off by inner tension or stress. When the blood circulation of the face improves, the blood circulation in the brain also increases. The body thereby increases the oxygen supply to the brain which ensures improved capabilities in particular situations. In situations where it is important for us that our brain function efficiently, there is no reason for our wanting to restrict the flow of blood in the head region.

If going red is a problem for you then it is useful to know that you cannot simply turn off the tendency to blush with a trick or something similar. If you give yourself the instruction: 'Don't go red', then you are giving yourself the impulse to turn red, because our brains do not process the word 'don't' in the same way as they do the words 'turn red'. The brain processes the words 'turn red' first and only then the 'don't'. This means that by giving the order 'don't turn red!' you first of all trigger off the impulse to blush and only afterwards halt this impulse with the word 'don't'. The same thing occurs when, for example, you read the words 'do not think of pink elephants'. If you do this you will probably start by thinking of pink elephants and then reject them on an inner level, eliminate them or paint them another colour. But to begin with you thought of pink elephants in order subsequently to be able to eliminate them.

Blushing frequently decreases if you stop trying to fight against it, if you accept that you are a human being who is just prone to blushing. You are somebody who blushes in the process of speaking. This is who you are and is part of you. If you can accept your blushing as part of your existence you will be more at ease with yourself and will stop being embarrassed or wanting to hide because of it. If you blush when speaking in front of others, then so be it. Another little tip: a participant who for a long time suffered from chronic blushing gave a quick-witted response to the words, 'But Janet, there's no need to blush!' said by a colleague. She replied, 'I'm sorry you don't like the colour of my face, Peter, but it's the only one I can do', and won the round 1:0, instead of wanting the ground to rise and swallow her up as she had on previous occasions.

The mere act of blushing may in itself be reason enough for you to fear speaking in front of a group. If this is the case with you, it may be useful to try the focusing exercise in Chapter 3.

Saying Something Stupid or Incorrect

'Stop talking rubbish. You're talking a load of nonsense!' Already as children we learnt that if you talk rubbish or say something stupid you will be ridiculed or perhaps even punished. 'That's just not acceptable!' 'I just don't want to appear stupid! Better to say nothing and bite my tongue than take the risk of saying something incorrect!' Rendered powerless by inner strait-jackets such as these, many women sit silently on the fringe of discussions and meetings. They do not dare to voice their opinions. Their fear that somebody could show their comments to be wrong or stupid is simply too great. And if they do take courage and start speaking, their opening sentence will usually begin with a self-deprecatory remark or a remark belittling themselves, such as 'I don't know, this may sound stupid, but ...' or 'I've just had a stupid idea ...'. Many people make a rule of only allowing themselves to speak in front of a group of people if their own thoughts are correct, logical and irrefutable. To put it the other way round, this means that they forbid themselves simply to think out loud or throw in random thoughts during a discussion, to speak spontaneously.

The inner rule 'I mustn't say anything stupid or incorrect!' is often closely connected to the rule 'I must always put in an excellent performance!' Many women who live and work with these inner restrictions put themselves (and sometimes also other people) under immense pressure to perform and to be perfect. They often experience work, achievement and ability as a battle waged against themselves and others. Every situation that involves one's own performance is experienced as a kind of test – and is accompanied by the relevant fear of being tested. This applies in particular to speeches delivered to an audience. For them it is a question of 'to be or not to be', of passing or failing. A 'wrong word' or a 'stupid remark' and the woman concerned already experiences the feeling of being written off by the listeners.

A 44-year-old art historian who acted as advisor to various museums and art galleries suffered from extreme stage fright when she had to give professional talks at exhibitions or to groups of colleagues. Although she was an expert in her field, she was afraid that she might make a mistake during the course of her speech. To get a date mixed up or pronounce a word incorrectly was in her eyes not just a mistake but almost a catastrophe.

> What I say must be correct and verifiable! After all, I've a long education behind me and people have a right to expect me to make precise references. I cannot afford to make mistakes in this job. It's just not an option. That's why I check all my references three or four times before giving a talk. Nevertheless I get nervous because it's so gruesome if a mistake slips out or a colleague realises that I've said something incorrect.

We invited this woman to try out a simple exercise designed to reduce the fear of making mistakes or making slips of the tongue. We asked her to hold a special kind of lecture in front of the group. A lecture in which there was not a single sensible sentence. In other words, this was about talking rubbish over a sustained period of time.

This proved to be the greatest challenge in the seminar for the art historian. She spoke normal words but strung them together to form completely nonsensical sentences about the history of art. It required great effort for her to overcome the fear of uttering her first stupid sentence. Prior to giving her speech she sat in front of the group and, in her words, 'sweated buckets'. After her first hesitant and awkward sentences her inner block began to dissolve and the rest of her speech was for her a joy to deliver. Her nonsense speech was recorded on video and subsequently played back to her. She saw and heard herself 'talking nonsense on purpose' for the first time in her adult life and, what is more, with others listening to and watching her.

After the exercise she reported that to begin with the situation had been extremely embarrassing for her and that she would have liked to have stopped. Yet through it she was able to discover what for her was the worst thing about speaking incorrectly in front of others and so was able to take a look behind the scenes of her inner rule of 'always having to be correct and perfect'. By giving herself this rule she had wanted to protect herself from the experience of failure:

> My worst nightmare is to make mistakes as a specialist. By that I mean somebody detecting that I haven't done my homework, that I have been sloppy. I always think that my reputation as an expert is on the line and that I can't afford to make any mistakes. I've studied and grafted for too long becoming what I am and have had to fight for the position in which I now work.

Behind her inner rule calling for perfection lay the 'nightmare' of no longer being regarded as an expert. Of course she knew that one or more mistakes or slips of the tongue would not lead to her downfall. Nevertheless every time she gave a speech she feared that her status as an expert would be undermined. At every public lecture her ability and competence were on the line. To pass or to fail – this was the test every time she made a speech.

By conducting the nonsense speech exercise she was practising what she wanted to avoid – failure, disaster and a large number of mistakes whilst speaking.

Many weeks after the seminar, at a reunion of former seminar participants, the art historian reported the changes she had undergone as a result of this exercise. The fear that she previously felt before speaking had diminished to such an extent that she could hardly sense it. She was much less frightened of making mistakes during her lectures, although she still prepared thoroughly for them. Furthermore, she was in the process of 'being a bit more laid back and not so overly serious', even having the courage to introduce humour into her talks.

This nonsense speech exercise is of course not intended to show women how they can talk rubbish in future but an exercise in breaking down women's rules about correctness and perfection, rules with which they hinder themselves.

It is only human to make mistakes and to admit to them calls for sympathy. We agree with Ingrid Steeger, who once said: 'It is our mistakes that makes us clever, and for this reason one is not enough!'

The 'er' in Speech

Superfluous and annoying sounds, like 'er', often slip off the tongue when people pause in brief thought whilst speaking. The speaker is trying to decide on the next word or sentence in these pauses in speech. Many people bridge these short pauses with this sort of utterance.

Just how many of these 'ers' slip out whilst speaking usually only becomes noticeable to some when they look at a video recording of their speaking. Often, because speakers are concentrating so intensely on what they are saying, the odd 'er' escapes unnoticed.

However, if the woman concerned knows that an 'er' slips out now and again, speaking becomes more difficult. She is now clearly aware of every 'er' she lets out, something that causes a hiccup in her rhythm or perhaps even throws her completely off balance.

The utterance of an 'er', an 'um' and other sounds is a habit that can have a reason. These sounds may serve the purpose of producing an uninterrupted flow of speech. Women (and men) who have experienced being interrupted before having been heard out tend towards a tense and hurried mode of speech. They want to get everything they have to say out as quickly as possible before somebody interrupts them. Whilst they pause between words to think, the letting out of an 'er' signals that they are not yet done.

The dismantling of inner rules and decrees contributes fundamentally to producing a calmer and less hurried manner of speaking. If the speaker allows herself to think in peace whilst making her speech, gives herself and the audience breaks, then the number of 'er'-type utterances often diminishes automatically of its own accord.

Furthermore, for women it is often important that they defend their right to speak and that they are able to make a stand against interrupters. If you are frequently interrupted try becoming forceful, looking the interrupting person straight in the eye, by way of body language signalling 'STOP, I'm not done yet!', 'Wait a second' or 'Please let me finish saying what I have to say' and thereby secure the space in which to carry on speaking. This can easily be practised in any such situation or in training.

Getting Stuck and Losing the Thread

If a speech is not read word for word off a script but is spoken freely it is possible that the connection between thoughts and sentences may not always be perfect. Even the most honed script is no guarantee against losing the thread when delivering a speech. (There are of course types of script that are more helpful and those that tend to confuse. A discussion of the type of script that is useful is to be found in Chapter 4, 'Winning People over Self-Confidently: Aids, Tips and Techniques'.)

A speech that is not read from a script is like a walk in the countryside. Getting bogged down may be compared to pausing briefly and consulting a map to reorient yourself or change direction. Why is it then that people fear getting bogged down during a speech so much?

It is this short moment of disorientation, which is often experienced as an eternity, that they hate so much. We have no control when it comes to getting stuck during a speech. We lose the thread, whether we like it or not. This gives rise to a feeling of helplessness and of not being in control.

In addition, losing the thread has negative connotations for many people. Getting stuck is a mistake, a failure and a sign of nervousness, fear and/or stupidity. Much of this emanates from our time at school. The teacher asked the pupils a question, to which someone stumbled through an answer. Or the recollection of having to go up to the blackboard in front of the whole class and explain something and getting stuck half way through and not knowing how to continue. Many adults still carry around with them the memory of such embarrassing experiences at school, and some situations can trigger off the recollection of what it felt like: your mind is swept clean and the fiendish laughter of your classmates rings shrilly in your ears. Getting stuck back then was associated with biting ridicule, bad marks or simply feelings of embarrassment. And some people still fear this today when they get stuck whilst speaking.

Also, many people's vision of what an ideal speech should look or sound like is false. They consider an ideal speech to be one in which the words flow, one which runs smoothly and uninterruptedly like a stream.

In actual fact, an exciting and effective speech is more like a wind that blows with different strengths. Sometimes it is more of a blustery storm and sometimes it is a light breeze. In between it dies down completely. A pause, an interruption in speech is not a mistake, but a necessary stillness of the wind, through which contrast and tension are achieved. Stillness and silence in the course of a speech do not of themselves constitute failure, and often have dramatic effect.

It is only the inner rule 'I must not get stuck!' that allows the breaking of the flow of speech to become a problem. The fear and the pressure to prevent exactly this happening causes the brief uncertainty of how to proceed to break out into an inner panic.

Instead of calmly looking for a starting point, the speaker activates the carousel of fear 'Oh no, I don't know how to continue!' With fear in her head and in her heart she now really cannot think of anything. In this way a little torn thread results in a complete blackout. The carousel is now turning faster and faster. Apparently nothing works any more.

In a state of being blocked, even well-meant tips like 'breathe in deeply!' are as good as useless. The only thing which really helps in this case is the dissolution of the blockage simply by letting be what happens to be: 'Okay. The thread is broken.' Full stop. And then you usually remember without the aid of a tip or trick how to continue.

When the fear of getting stuck abates, the entire manner of speech usually changes. As a result of their fear of losing the thread, many people try to express what they have to say as quickly as possible. When losing the thread no longer appears a problem, most people talk much more slowly and spiritedly. They allow themselves the time to think and come into interaction with the audience. Another tip: use your broken thread to involve and activate your listeners. Ask for help: 'Where did I leave off?'

To show the participants of our training sessions how to deal calmly with their blackouts we have developed an exercise which provokes broken threads. Whilst speaking, a participant is shown words on cardboard boards which she is asked to incorporate sensibly into what she is saying. To integrate words like 'ketchup', 'Christmas celebration' or 'trend-setter' creatively into a speech can easily cause the speaker to get lost. The aim of this exercise is calmly to pick up the thread again.

Heckling and Being Attacked by the Audience

Friendly smiles, nods of assent and applause are the kind of reactions we wish to see in an audience. What, however, if there is no approval and the only response from the audience is an icy silence or obvious rejection?

What I fear most is being rebuffed. If I am talking and people roll their eyes in dismay, then I immediately become nervous. The worst thing I can imagine happening is being whistled at or having people shout 'shut up!' at me.

This is the account of a woman who for several years has been working in the field of communal politics. She continues:

> If I am speaking in front of people who I know hold the same opinion as I do, I'm nervous but not really scared. As soon as there are differences of opinion, for example in a discussion, my knees immediately start shaking and I can barely say a word.

There is not only the real possibility of reaping laurels when giving a speech but also that of disagreement and rejection. Most of the time vehement disapproval on the part of the audience exists only in the speaker's imagination. Women who fear being booed or whistled at whilst speaking have seldom experienced this themselves. Yet merely imagining that something like this could happen is for many enough to terrify them, since they would break their rule 'I must get my point across! The listeners must not reject me!'

We offer an exercise in our training in which the participants get to experience unmistakable rejection by an audience whilst speaking. The degree of severity of rebuff is determined by the participant herself. This ranges from imperceptible shakings of the head and whispering amongst the audience to laughing, heckling and noisy exits during the speech. Every participant who stands in the crossfire of the protest is experimenting with her own reactions. What kind of attacks from the audience is she capable of ignoring, how might she react and what kind of rejection proves to be particularly painful for her? Some people develop very useful combat strategies or discover that an intense attack by the audience really gets their backs up, really gets their speech going. Everybody goes through the same thing: they discover that they can all withstand being attacked. This may sound strange at first. But most women who are afraid of rejection and attacks believe that they would not be able to bear being rejected by people. After the exercise many discovered that being rebuffed by an audience did not have the disastrous consequences they had previously assumed it would. Most women were surprised at their own robustness and eagerness for a quarrel. At the same time many discovered that there is no general 'correct' or 'always effective' way of dealing with rejections and attacks. Sometimes it is more helpful in terms of the discussion as a whole simply to ignore a heckle. There are however situations in which it is definitely right and important to deal with a heckle or flatly to contradict it.

The way in which speakers deal with rejection or attacks does of course depend on their personalities. Some women in our seminars discovered that they are definitely capable of making little ironic comments in the course of their speech. Others turned out to be virtuosos of indignation and loud rebuke. It is also the case that a spontaneous and reasonable reaction to heckles and attacks can only develop if thought, and in particular creativity, are not blocked by inner proscriptions.

WOMEN'S FEAR OF SPEAKING: FEAR WITH A SYSTEM

In this section we are going to question: is there a common breeding ground for women's fear of speaking?

We found that the upbringing as a woman represents the foundation for further stumbling-blocks:

- the inner conviction of being inferior
- perfectionism
- the desire for external recognition

Apart from this heavily socially dependent reason for the fear of speaking by women there are often also individual experiences that are established in childhood. We will introduce you to some of them under the title 'Skeletons in the Closet'. Perhaps you will recognise yourself in one or another description and will get to take a step closer to discovering the reasons for your own fear of speaking.

The Old 'Women's Corset'

To begin with we will consider the fear of speaking by women as a social and cultural problem. The public appearance and speaking of women is, from a historical point of view, quite a recent achievement. 'Women must be silent in the community' has, as a biblical imperative, become outdated, and yet the reality in lecture theatres, conference rooms or club houses often makes it seem as if this rule is still very much in force. The rules of conduct by which women are to behave vary from woman to woman and differ in the degree to which they are ingrained more than we think. Some of them can interfere to such an extent that speaking becomes a problem. Above all the rule 'Be quiet and reserved!' A good girl is not forward. On the contrary: she is reserved and quiet.

If two women draw a deep breath simultaneously in a seminar this usually results in the 'after-you-effect'. Each smiles at the other and says 'you first'. 'No, you first!' Just don't push in! This rule is deeply ingrained in many people. Letting others take the word often means that they don't get round to speaking at all. However friendly and polite such conduct may be, it is also obstructive if it is turned into a strict rule. Because it means that some women present at a discussion are only ever catching air. Because they fear pushing in, taking up space, 'taking up room' they withdraw completely and are silent.

A further rule that can cause women difficulty in speaking is 'be modest!', and women find it difficult to talk about their ability and competence. It comes as no surprise that one of the most difficult exercises in our training is for a woman to talk positively about herself for three minutes.

The aim of this exercise is not to exaggerate, to brag or even to act the 'strong man', but to report on one's existing abilities. No more, no less. But nevertheless the exercise is mostly considered to be embarrassing: for many women to be asked to evaluate themselves and then openly to talk about it verges on arrogance (and this is bad and is known to precede the fall).

So women tend to be masters at belittling themselves, at hiding their light under a bushel, at playing down their abilities, rather than finding enjoyment in showing themselves in a good light.

Making a rule of modesty often hinders showing oneself as competent in front of others, and at the same time prevents one from experiencing the joy of success. Women who set themselves this rule often start speaking with an apology ('Unfortunately I am not a very experienced speaker ...') and end with a belittling remark ('That's all I have to say, that's it'). The possible applause is curtailed by the quick escape from the speaker's desk. This is because women not only fear possible booing after a speech, but become just as embarrassed if they receive thunderous applause, because this offends their modesty rule: to receive applause, to taste one's own success, to give oneself praise is forbidden. This false modesty frequently contributes to the experience of not being taken seriously and increases in a double sense one's own feeling of failure.

Another rule that is specific to women and manifests itself in the way that women act when speaking is 'Conform and be supportive'. The role of a woman is to listen sympathetically, to agree, to echo what others say or ask questions, with it being considered offensive if they have their own opinion. This can have such a far-reaching effect that women completely forget to develop their own opinion, let alone stand by their opinion or assert it in front of others. A woman in a seminar described this precisely: 'I don't know what I want. For years I have done nothing but be ivy wrapped around my husband.'

Apart from gender-specific rules that refer to restraint, modesty and conformity, another fundamental rule plays a role in causing fear of speaking: *a woman must be beautiful!* Beauty is what we have all learnt: ideal measurements, ideal weight, smiling and wearing the latest fashions.

Speaking in public or professional situations is often connected with being seen by important men. And it is precisely this which causes distress for many women: to be seen and judged firstly on the basis of their outward appearance and then only later on the content of their speech. Women who speak in public often get to experience this. The video recordings that we did during our seminars brought to light the core of some women's fear of speaking: 'I mustn't talk because I am ugly', 'because I am too fat', 'because I've got buckteeth'. On taking a closer look, the fear of speaking reveals itself as a fear of showing ourselves because of not living up to the common ideal of beauty or because of thinking that we do not.

Upbringing turns out for many women who fear speaking to be the main reason for their insecurity. Even if the traditional 'women's corset' has been loosened in recent history, it has left more or less visible constrictions. We live in a society in which men's values and strength, ability to assert themselves, drive to succeed, and so on, rule supreme and in which women are rated inferior. This external belittlement is carried around by many as a internalised contempt for women and is frequently the cause of an underlying insecurity, which we describe as a further breeding ground for fear of speaking in what follows.

The Inner Conviction of Being Inferior

Fear of speaking is often associated with the fear of being the centre of attention, as has already been mentioned in the previous section. If we take a closer look at this scene and the associated fears, women often report feelings such as piercing looks or of being undressed, feeling naked, completely unprotected and at the mercy of others, and of everybody's being able to see through them to the core of their being. What could then come to light is mostly a small, insignificant, stupid and ugly being, that has to be hidden from everybody, as described in the following quote: 'I'm scared of being insignificant, of no value. Scared of people finding out how small, stupid and barmy I am.'

Fear of speaking manifests itself as an expression of a general inner insecurity about one's own worth, one's own strength, one's own effectiveness. We were surprised to find just how many women live with this internalised contempt for women, with the conviction that they are inferior. Many women who participated in speech training (to the onlooker) come across as being self-confident, competent women. But inside they die a thousand deaths and their low self-esteem appears to be in constant danger of being exposed. In one of our sessions a successful woman expressed this with the following words:

> The others are cleverer than I am, and if I don't watch out when I'm talking they'll also realise that I'm stupid. I'm more stupid than the others, that's clear. I find this sad, but that's how it is, there's nothing I can do about it. The fact in itself is clear. But they must not notice.

Many women occupy themselves with hiding this part of their character, which they feel is worthless. The central rule 'It mustn't be obvious that I am inferior!' is backed up by many further prohibitions, like: I must not

– appear unsure of myself
– blush
– say something wrong
– ask a question

Concealment can lead as far as to making the person in question invisible and inaudible, as if she were wearing a magic cape. One woman was so deeply caught up in this process that she avoided expressing anything at all: she had been silent for years, only wore plain or black clothes and had a lifeless facial expression. All these strategies were supposed to help her protect her inner, vulnerable self according to the maxim 'If I don't act, then it's not possible for me to act wrongly.'

At the end of our workshops we frequently get to hear: 'At the beginning I thought I was the only one who feared speaking and that everybody else had come to the wrong place.' This phenomenon is a result of your own insecurity which leads you to think everybody else is competent but you and only you are the person who is a failure. When it comes to ourselves we are extremely critical and merciless in our judgement. This is why many women find it hard to believe that it's really them they are seeing when they see themselves on video. One woman writes: '... the most overwhelming thing was to see myself. This charming woman on the video, who spoke at ease, without expletives, often pausing and looking directly at the listeners, seemed a complete stranger to me.'

So it is that many find it difficult to exchange the inferior picture they have of themselves for the actual, real picture. 'That can't be me', said one woman after seeing herself on video. 'My friend always tells me that on the outside I don't make a catastrophic impression, but I just never believe her, I just thought she wanted to spare my feelings.' Often the conviction of being inferior is so persistent that, as is apparent from the above example, even praise and encouragement barely have a chance. This inner attitude towards oneself is a central breeding ground for fear of speaking, although the next one contributes towards it to the same extent.

Perfectionism

It is not unusual for an inner desire for perfection to spring from the feeling of being inferior. Inner rules are meant to serve the purpose of changing one's own person, deemed inadequate, into an ideal: I must

- not make any mistakes
- always be relaxed
- be something special
- know everything etc.

The compulsion arises to be outstanding, without weaknesses, simply perfect. This is why even the smallest mistake can become a source of danger, since it puts at risk the supportive framework of one's own perfection. Little slips sometimes transform themselves into huge catastrophes, as one woman put it: 'If the first words of a speech don't elegantly slip off my tongue, everything is ruined – then I just run through the rest, so that it's all over quickly.'

What is being striven for is total perfection, behind which lies the hope: if I am perfect (that means competent, good, right, attractive and so on) then I'm acceptable, I would feel that I belonged and everything would be okay. Only there is no such thing as perfection. The quest for perfection is comparable to chasing one's own shadow: it is before your eyes and yet you can never reach it, because it could always have been better. So from the very beginning we are doomed to failure. Because we want to achieve something that is not possible we feel we have failed. To make matters worse, this failure does not just occur on an internal level but is, as already explained, provoked by extremely high achievement expectations. Through the internal pressure the 'real failure' (meaning a blackout, stuttering or losing the thread) is mostly pre-programmed, and the vicious circle of one's own evaluation deepens even further: 'The next time I will just have to be better prepared/do another course in public speaking, seeing as I act so stupidly ...'

A further factor which arises as a result of the above two, is:

The Yearning for External Recognition or:
The Fear of Losing Popularity

Women are brought up to relate to others. They look after men, children and parents needing care, and in addition they often engage in social jobs. It is their job to look after others – in conversations too. Women have, as the linguist Senta Trömel Plötz describes, a 'co-operative style of speech': they ask questions, listen, follow others, confirm and seek confirmation, summarise and rarely interrupt, and if they do so, it is mainly for the purpose of being supportive. A woman's role dictates a type of 'relationship language', in which everything depends on understanding others and establishing co-operative agreements. In most cases the atmosphere is more important than establishing a hierarchy or following through the points of view. If you ask women why they are scared of stating their opinion, the most common answer is that they are worried about being rejected. The worst thing is not being liked by anyone, and this is what would happen if they gave a differing opinion, if they gave up their co-operative support work and made themselves the centre of attention. Many women therefore prefer to conform to the rules of others at the expense of losing their assertiveness and independence. They only feel valuable as people if there are others there who confirm that they are.

Because of their dependency on relationships and on external confirmation, women who fear speaking are in danger of losing their self-esteem: a disparaging glance, a critical word and the rug of their self-esteem is pulled from under their feet. This means that they often have finely attuned antennae that register their surroundings and incoming signals. This radar system is set off at the smallest sign, and is unfortunately calibrated to failure: 'I have failed if somebody raises an eyebrow. It doesn't take much. Or if somebody makes a reserved impression, then I've also failed. That's why I constantly fail.'

In this or a similar way, women who are afraid of speaking confirm their inner catastrophic idea of not being likeable. This is where a circle is formed, which is described by one woman as follows:

I think the worst thing is for my achievements not to be recognised. I'm not allowed to make any mistakes for that would be to fail. For me achievement is strongly linked to love. Very close, only above it. If I don't achieve something, I'm worthless. I must always perform at 150 per cent, for the worst thing is not to be loved.

And it is to precisely this that the majority of inner rules that are connected to fear of speaking lead back.

Apart from the mentioned breeding ground for fear of speaking, there is a further one, which can mostly be found in one's own childhood:

The 'Skeletons in the Closet'

What we mean by this is all the unpleasant, embarrassing or painful experiences that women who fear speaking carry around inside them. For the most part well hidden, they ferment, and it is often in childhood, 'where the body is buried', where the causes of the fear of speaking are to be found. In our advisory and training sessions we dug up some experiences from which women had learned lessons for life: learned to hold their tongue, to say nothing of themselves, never to venture into the centre of attention and so on.

For example, one woman spoke of how she 'always had to be special' when she was a little girl, was showered with attention and was always dressed up despite the fact that it made her feel extremely uncomfortable. Since that time she has detested any situation which involves being looked at by others. There are also experiences which contain the exact opposite. One woman told us 'I wasn't supposed to be there. I think it was early on that I realised that I was unwanted and a burden to my parents, and so I just pretended that I wasn't really there.' Now an adult, she still found it difficult to take up space, to make her presence felt, 'to take up room' through speech and body. The deeply ingrained rule from her childhood 'I must act as if I weren't really here' continued to have an effect and caused a block when she spoke in public.

A string of other painful childhood and teenage experiences stem from school time: being exposed in front of the whole class, laughed at or humiliated, harassed when having to sing or recite a poem in front of classmates. Never speak in front of a group again! Definitely not say anything about myself! The very feeling 'of being served up on a plate', avoid it! – these are typical rules that originate in painful experiences at school. A Turkish woman told of her experience of always being an outsider in her class and how this had made her suffer from a feeling of loneliness and alienation. To escape this inner conflict, she developed the rule of conforming whatever the cost: 'Just don't be different and stand out because of it!' She made this her highest precept, and it blocked her in all situations in which she would have liked to have expressed a different opinion.

Another woman attributed her fear of speaking to her relationship with her mother. She was a well-known politician, who made regular television appearances and gave impressive speeches. 'Don't turn out like your mother!' was something she had already resolved early on, because the desire to compare herself to her was always connected with the feeling of not being able to measure up to her standard. That this was the reason for her fear of speaking – the danger of being compared to her mother when speaking in public – only became clear to her later on.

These and other kinds of individual 'skeletons in the closet' are numerous: experiences which are suppressed or forgotten because they are unpleasant but continue to ferment on an inner level. Fear of speaking then often manifests itself as the tip of the iceberg. If you want to deal with painful experiences of the kind that you have been carrying around with you for a long time then it may be sensible not to do this on your own, but to get professional help. Also, if you sense that you are not getting any further with your self-help, that you find yourself going around in circles or just marking time when it comes to your problems, we would like to encourage you to seek support in the way of therapy. The thought of having to deal with 'skeletons in the closet' oneself may appear unpleasant, but it is well worth taking this step. For when dealing with psychological damage we are not concerned with opening old wounds but with giving them the chance to heal. A client described the uncovering of her old experiences like this: 'Because I took a closer look at my hermetically-sealed vault it was as if I had opened a door and let the air reach the corpse that was fermenting away. And it was only through the light and the air that it could really begin to decompose.'

How Inner Rules Increase Fear: The Vicious Circle of Fear

Gender-specific upbringing and the feeling of inferiority it gives rise to, perfectionism and the desire for recognition, as well as the painful childhood experiences just described may all form the basis for the fear of speaking.

We would again like to clarify how the process of 'making-rules-for-oneself' increases the fear of speaking. The breeding grounds for fear of speaking described in the preceding section are the basis for the process of making rules for oneself. In situations where inner rules are activated, the 'inner fire' begins to blaze. Fear, pressure or lack of self-confidence can set a circle of fear of speaking in motion, like a vicious circle, which fuels itself. For example it can take the following form: by making rules for ourselves we put ourselves under pressure on an inner level.

This internal pressure, the feeling of stress or fear, makes us tense and increases the possibility of running into trouble whilst speaking: we collect negative speech experiences like blushing, stammering, losing the thread, blacking out and so on.

These experiences can lead to our avoiding situations in which we find the experience of speaking stressful: we prefer to remain silent, back out, leave the speaking to others.

Evasion is often the reason why we lack practice. We do not 'train' ourselves to speak as much, have fewer experiences and have less experience of success.

Lack of practice contributes towards a greater lack of self-confidence and to an increase in stress and fear in speech situations.

This vicious circle of fear in turn strengthens the inner process of making oneself rules ('I just have to say more', '... get rid of my fear at last', 'I mustn't make a fool of myself again' and so on) so that the whole system stabilises itself. In this way we contribute towards making the corset tighter, making ourselves feel even more inferior or thinking that we should be even more perfect. We feel more keenly that we are dependent on external recognition, and bury our old skeletons even deeper in the closet. Is there an emergency exit? Yes, in the same way that you are able to inflame the described circle of fear, you can stop it. Start by putting a stop to making rules for yourself (even the instruction 'I mustn't make rules any more!' is an instruction ...).

What could this mean? If you stopped making rules for yourself, you could start becoming conscious of what simply exists. This could mean saying goodbye to your own desired ideal and consciously confronting the normal everyday reality of your own existence. This would also mean taking a risk, since it would involve becoming aware of your own real limitations, your actual failures, weaknesses, flaws, habits and imperfections. To perceive oneself lovingly with all the feelings of pain, sorrow, shame, anger, despair, helplessness etc. that this involves means winning back contact to oneself, giving oneself up to the liveliness of one's emotions. And it is part of the diversity of life that not only the beautiful and pleasant feelings belong in that list, but also those that we would usually rather ignore, above all fear. The moment we perceive our own normality it becomes clear that evaluations of good and bad dissolve, and with them the self-imposed compulsion to be different from the way we are and the prohibition to feel what we feel.

We want to encourage you to take the risk of unlacing your self-constructed corset right up to the point where you show yourself in your own individual shape and richness, the way you are.

3   Developing the Ability to Feel at Ease: Solutions and Exercises

Now that we have described how the fear of speaking manifests itself, how it comes about, what the process of giving ourselves instructions triggers off and which instructions in particular can affect women, we would like in the second part of this book to offer you practical advice on how to break down your fear of speaking.

Most of the participants in our seminars wish they had a button they could press to switch off their fear of speaking. Fear can be such a tiresome and unpleasant feeling that they would do anything to get rid of it: do a handstand, swallow a pill or mumble a magic formula, the main thing being that it would help. That this button does not exist is a disappointment, but nevertheless there is a rule that should be taken note of when trying to break down fear:

Trying to avoid the fear leads to reinforcing it.
Confronting fear leads to its dissolution.

Avoiding Fear

Avoiding fear means avoiding situations in which you will have to speak; not thinking of worrying situations, better to watch television, to ignore the fear, to coax yourself or pull yourself together and so on. These everyday strategies provide temporary relief. That is their advantage and that is why most people are familiar with them. If you consider them on a long-term basis, they merely stabilise the fear rather than actually reducing it since they only avoid it instead of actually working on it. Nevertheless, because of their short-term effectiveness, they may be useful in certain situations, where we would otherwise, for example, work ourselves up into a state of fear. They are to be compared to a first-aid kit that is carried around in case of emergency, with which it is possible neither to heal ourselves completely nor to prevent accidents from happening in the first place. We will attempt to make you more aware of some of these evasive manoeuvres at the end of this overview.

Speaking Ability

Another possible way of reducing fear is actively to practise when you are in these worrying situations. Fear may arise when you feel that you cannot deal with a difficult situation, that you simply are not up to it. For some participants in our training sessions the actual reason for their fear of speaking is a matter of their not knowing how to give a speech in front of a group of people. They lack the practice, perhaps because they have avoided putting themselves in situations where they are required to speak. For these women their level of fear diminishes in accordance with the increase of their ability and competence. This experience can sometimes be gained just by doing some exercises and, by means of these, acquiring basic speech know-how. In the fourth chapter we will introduce you to aids, tips and techniques which we consider to be helpful in this connection.

Confronting Fear

The fear of speaking often does not stop automatically, even if you are good at it. Proof of this is the many brilliant speakers who attend our sessions because, despite their ability, they still feel afraid about speaking. They also wish they could break down their fear, not on a short-term basis but on a long-term one. The first step is to stop giving yourself the instruction 'The fear has to go!' The methods of dismantling fear that we are going to introduce you to are about confronting the fear: looking it in the face, exploring and feeling it, becoming aware of it, of what it is like to tolerate it without pushing it away as you are accustomed to doing. This means putting yourself in worrying situations instead of avoiding them. We will show you in the section 'On the Way to Feeling More at Ease' how these methods can help you to cope with and ultimately break down your fear.

To summarise, opposite is an overview of the three described ways of dealing with fear:

Avoiding Fear	Speaking Ability	Confronting Fear

— — — — — — — *Help, Tips and Techniques* — — — — — — —

I	II	III
Avoidance	Brakes applied by Nervousness	Greeting Fear
		Accepting Awareness
Situations that give rise to fear	Rhetorical know-how	– in the imagination – in reality
Diversion	Practice	Through 'focusing' dismantle the inner rules
Fleeing		
Pulling oneself together		
Calming/Anaesthetising		
Positive Thinking		
Leads to short-term relief – in the long term the fear is reinforced.	Leads to greater personal competence, is of practical help in speech situations, can contribute to breaking down fear.	Leads in the short term to more intensive experience of fear – in the long term to the breaking down of fear. At first the experience of fear can increase, in the long term it dissipates.

AVOIDING FEAR

When we ask the participants of our seminars which strategies they use to dismantle their fear of speaking, we are offered an array of methods and tricks resulting from their unpleasant experiences of this fear. Some say that the best method of dealing with the fear is not to put themselves in situations where they have to speak in the first place. Others mention cleverly devised evasive manoeuvres such as 'If I blush, I pinch my hand hard so that I concentrate on the pain and not on my red face, then it goes away of its own accord.' Or 'I always think: it's not going to kill you, whatever happens, you're not going to die!' Some women prepare themselves thoroughly because of their fear, hold on to a biro or put their shaky hands in their pockets. Others recommend tranquillisers or practise positive thinking ('You're great, everybody is going to find what you have to say interesting, it will run smoothly ...' and so on).

To the question of how satisfied they were with their strategies for alleviating their fear most participants replied: not particularly. They are helpful at that particular moment, they are better than nothing, but their experience is that it is necessary to use them on every new occasion because the fear itself did not change fundamentally.

This is precisely the case with these 'evasive methods'. Their only purpose is to stop the fear, at any rate on a short-term basis, by trying to avoid it. At first we can feel relief, we are distracting ourselves, thinking of something else, avoiding worrying situations – but in the long term it is precisely this evasive behaviour that allows fear to become chronic: every time we avoid a situation the fear deepens, we make it more concrete. Often this results in 'fear of fear' – we are scared of feeling scared, of the bodily consequences of fear, and feel the experiencing of fear as being itself the actual catastrophe. In this way evasive behaviour maintains the fear as it is, with the fear in turn encouraging the evasive behaviour. This vicious circle can severely restrict the number of situations into which individuals will allow themselves to enter and step by step takes away the likelihood of their being tested by situations that give rise to fear.

The short-term feeling of relief that kicks in when these 'evasive methods' are used is only perceptible in the initial stage of feeling fear. If the experience of fear is full-blown, strategies employed that are supposed to banish it tend to increase the level of fear. The fight against fear increases the internal pressure and stokes the flames, and the thoughts 'I mustn't be so scared – but I am – but I'm not allowed to be scared ...' turn in ever tighter circles. The consequence of all this is that the person not only feels fear, but is also involved in an inner conflict which causes the tension to rise.

To recapitulate: avoiding fear can in the short term be a relief, but in the long term it leads to the fear's being reinforced.

We would now like to introduce you to some strategies that deal with this. In the process we will differentiate between two ways of avoiding fear –

1. Avoiding situations that trigger fear.

2. Avoiding the inner awareness of fear.

Avoiding Situations that Trigger Fear

The most obvious strategies are those that involve the attempt to avoid speaking at all:

– not attending discussions or parties

– dodging oral examinations

– preferring to deal with everything in writing

– not forming one's own opinion

– sitting apathetically when colleagues are having a discussion

– making no telephone calls

– giving others the space to speak by listening quietly, and putting this down to politeness

People's attempts at evasive behaviour are not always recognisable: people who look at the ceiling when talking because they are afraid of eye contact; others who talk their audience to death in order to avoid questions or harsh criticism; others who fear nothing more than being boring and avoid this by attempting to appear lively and witty; or those people who prepare themselves 200 per cent and spend the nights before the speech learning it perfectly off by heart, scared as they are of making mistakes or losing the thread. These strategies too are evasive manoeuvres to counteract fear, and this list only represents a small selection of innumerable possibilities to get out of these fear-producing situations.

Avoiding the Inner Awareness of Fear

It is not only possible to avoid the fear externally, but also internally, by suppressing the feeling of fear through ignoring it, fleeing, distracting and 'anaesthetising' oneself, and so on, as the following examples show.

Narcotics

The feeling of fear can be neutralised through the use of tranquillisers, nicotine, alcohol or food. In older books on speaking, written by the successful instructors of the day, you can find recommendations of the following kind: 'Drink a small glass of cognac before you get up to speak.' Alcohol, as is well known, loosens the tongue – and in the long term it leads to addiction, as all narcotics do, because its regular consumption gives you the feeling that you would not be able to cope without it. But it is rare to see somebody in an intoxicated state managing to be convincing to their audience.

Diversion

Instead of thinking of the speech to be held tomorrow and allowing oneself to feel scared at the thought of it, many people distract themselves by reading newspapers, watching television, thinking of their approaching holiday, cleaning the flat, writing letters, and so on. This kind of evasive behaviour is also recommended in the book on speaking just mentioned, presented as a means of dismantling the fear of it: 'If you already know your subject, try and distract yourself by thinking of other things.' Another speech trainer recommends that you concentrate on the tips of your fingers instead of on your heartbeat and offers finger shaking exercises to make you aware of your own fingertips. Here again the strategy is to avoid the experience of fear. These strategies are probably harmless, but their value is doubtful.

Pulling Yourself Together

Instead of distracting themselves, some people begin to tell themselves off: 'What nonsense, stop making such a fuss, get a grip ...'

Ordering oneself not to feel fear, gritting one's teeth, not making such a fuss can in the short term lead to suppression of the feeling of fear, but in the long term it causes an additional conflict: apart from the fear, we are also plagued by the anger of not being able to order the fear just to go away. The best tip we found in speech books on dismantling the fear of speaking was the maxim 'Never experience nervousness again': 'Step 10: Keep your composure whatever the situation!' Right then, on a count of three ...

Positive Thinking

Positive thinking is a good strategy along the path to success. If worship of success is obstructed, however, by doubt and fear it can give rise to an 'inner slinging match'. For example like this: instead of telling themselves off, some people use the opposing strategy. They think positive incantations to themselves in order to suppress the fear: 'Everything will work out', 'I won't be scared, I'll speak freely and easily.'

At the time these self-addressed instructions are thought, they convey a feeling of having control over one's own fear. What is so important is not what one tells oneself, but the fact that one says something and believes in the effectiveness of this formula. You could for example say 'abracadabra', if we were able to ingrain the conviction in you that it is precisely this formula that can break down your fear. What has an effect and leads to a momentary reduction of the feeling of fear is the fact that at the very moment you mumble the formula you stop yourself from getting worked up into a state of fear. You stop doubting yourself, stop picturing catastrophic disaster scenes or telling yourself: 'Nothing is allowed to go wrong.' For a short while you have the feeling that you have mastered your fear, that you have got it under control. For a moment this is a relief – but that is all.

Even if the use of some methods is questionable, they can have a short-term effect and that is why they are so popular. But any strategy that is based on the maxim 'stage fright – away with you!' must at first be distrusted. The breaking-down of fear leads through the path of fear. The paths that lead around the fear do not touch the fear, but let it remain as it is. To break down the fear is to confront it. In the next section we would like to encourage you to do this – step by step.

ON THE WAY TO FEELING MORE AT EASE: CONFRONTING FEAR

In this section we describe to you our strategy for getting to the bottom of your fear, welcoming it with open arms and ultimately breaking it down.

As already shown, the fear of speaking originates from giving yourself instructions on how you must speak or how those listening must be or must not be. The aim is to stop giving yourself instructions. On an inner level you achieve more peace of mind and composure if you learn to accept and value your exterior circumstances, your own feelings and your abilities. This is an invitation and encouragement to set yourself personal goals and to throw all your energy into achieving them. This attempt is about exploring where you stand and what you would like to change.

Start by holding up your fear to intense scrutiny:

- What kind of situations trigger off the fear of speaking?

- What kind of instructions do you give yourself in speech situations?

- How can you deal with your physical symptoms of fear?

At the end we will introduce you to 'focusing'. By using this method you can stop yourself from putting yourself under pressure by laying down inner rules for yourself.

Let us begin with the external catalysts of fear.

What Triggers the Fear of Speaking: The Background of Fear

To begin with we would like to invite you to get to the bottom of your external catalysts of fear. Often women in particular play down their speech inhibitions by for example saying 'I am just a quiet, modest woman', or 'I just can't express myself.' This negative self-image combines with the thought 'and that can't be changed anyway'. On taking a closer look you discover that your fear of speaking is linked to particular external conditions. For example, when you are on the sofa talking to your friend you are a very lively conversationalist, or during a marital dispute with your husband you can argue back perfectly well.

Often women attending our workshops who do the following exercise discover that, contrary to their expectations, they do not experience fear in particular situations. One participant at a professional training session was assigned the task of being the presenter of a small group and introducing the results to a large group on a board. If the organiser of this presentation exercise had already assigned this task to her in the morning she would have had enough time to work herself up into a state of fear. Another participant told of how a couple of colleagues suddenly pressed her into saying a few words of praise to her boss. In the offices of her agency, that is, in business situations, she was a convincing speaker. But in this personal context of the celebration she lost all sovereignty over her mind whilst speaking and would have liked to have been swallowed up by the ground because of her 'stumbling over her words'. To say something personal was 'sheer horror'.

What does the background of your fear look like? You can discover something about it through the following exercise.

Exercise: 'The Background of Fear'

Make some time for yourself, make yourself comfortable, close your eyes if you feel like it and remind yourself one after another, of two speech situations:

1. A situation in which you had to speak in which you felt comfortable, which may even have been a source of pleasure.

2. A situation in which you had to speak that made you frightened or in which you felt uncomfortable, tense or nervous.

Replay both scenes like an inner film and make a conscious note of everything that connects you to them. The following questions might prompt you:

– Which situations have you chosen?
  (Group discussion? Speech? Discussion? Dispute?
  Private or professional situations? Examination?)

– Which inner images emerge?
  (Participating people? Number of people? Gender? Position?
  Gestures and facial expressions? The way the room was laid out?)

– What can you hear?
  (Background noises? Other voices? Your own voice?)

– What kind of mood can you detect?
  (In the room? In yourself? In others?)

– How do you feel towards the participating people?
  (Equal? Indifferent? Negative?)

- What do you want to achieve with what you have to say?
  (To be seen or heard? To convince? To impress?
  To produce an effect? To assert yourself? To establish contact?)
- When do you feel most at ease or most uncomfortable?
  (Before you speak? Whilst you are speaking? Afterwards?
  At a particular moment?)
- Which of the following conditions essentially contribute to your
  inner reaction (fear or pleasure)?

Through this closer observation you may be able to isolate certain conditions that lead to your feeling uncomfortable in particular speech situations and at ease in others. Which factors contribute to your fear, that is, what the background of your fear of speaking looks like, vary from case to case.

Let us take a step further in from the external conditions that give rise to fear and look at what happens on an inner level at such stressful moments. In the following we would like to familiarise you with the method of 'thinking out loud', which enables you to become aware of your own thoughts, attitudes or evaluations.

The Inner Commentary:
Thoughts that Put the Speaker under Pressure

Without being aware of it, a constant burbling stream of thought runs through our heads, an inner commentary that even in everyday situations accompanies our own actions like a background murmur. Whilst I am writing this, this is what I am saying to myself: 'The pen has a strange groove – just like my toothbrush – the planes are really loud again today – can one say "A river runs downwards"? Oh God, it's already three o'clock – why can't I write more quickly ...'

Some of the thoughts are banal, associative, unimportant – some of them are very informative and are internal rules that play a central role in the emergence of fear.

The purpose of the following exercise is to get to the bottom of your own thought processes and the rules that are contained in them.

Exercise: 'Thinking Out Loud'

Put yourself in an unpleasant situation in which you have to speak again – perhaps the same one as in the previous exercise, perhaps a more recent one that you remember. Replay the scene again in front of your inner eye and stop the film at the point where you feel your fear or your discomfort the most. Now direct your attention to your mind: what kind of inner rules are you registering? Listen to your internal dialogue that simultaneously flows inside you and write down the sentences without assessing them, even if you find them trivial, embarrassing or absurd.

As already described in Chapter 2 you can tell when you are giving yourself instructions. Apart from the obvious formulations like 'should', 'ought', 'must not' there are further characteristics which point to imperatives. With the help of the following list you can examine your protocol of the previous experiment 'Thinking out loud' for such formulations:

This is How You Recognise Your Rules

- *Formulations of an absolute kind*

  'really', 'absolute', 'no way' , 'completely' etc.
  For example:
  'Today I really must open my mouth!'
  'Absolutely nothing came across in my speech today!'
  'That carping critic is totally ignorant!'

- *Generalisations*

  'always', 'all', 'nobody', 'never' etc.
  For example:
  'My boss always has to interrupt!'
  'I'm never asked to lead the presentation!'
  'Nobody really listened to me!'

When making an assessment you should note that with both of these linguistic categories not every statement that contains a generalisation is necessarily an instruction, for example: 'All students must pass an examination in order to receive a degree.' In this case only a particular matter of fact is established.

- *Adjectives that are strongly negative*

  'bad', 'awful', 'catastrophic', 'dreadful' etc.
  For example:
  'Oh, it would be really dreadful if I had ...'
  'It's bad that they always have to whisper to each other!'
  'The main thing is that I forget today's catastrophic performance quickly!'

- *Blasphemy*

  'Oh my God!', What the hell!', 'For Christ's sake!' etc.
  For example:
  'For Christ's sake, can't he speak a little more slowly!'
  'Oh God, what was the name of the author of that book!'

- *Swear words*

  'Crap', 'Bloody', 'Moron' etc.
  For example:
  'By the time I've got through this crap!'
  'These bloody foreign words that I don't understand!'
  'Does the moron think he can do this better?!'

- *Sentences containing*

  'I hope ...' or 'hopefully' which conceal fear.
  For example:
  'I hope the examination runs smoothly!'
  'Hopefully they won't interrupt me with as many questions as they
  did last time!'

- *Sentences that can logically be adjoined with*

  '... and that's bad/awful', or '... and that mustn't happen!'
  For example:
  'Just don't let me blush... that would be awful!'
  'Nobody would be interested in what I had to say again ... and that
  would be terrible!'
  'If they start noticing how insecure I feel – that's bad!'

You immediately come across your inner rules if you ask yourself the
question: 'What is the worst thing in such a speech situation for me?'

The first step towards breaking down your fear is to uncover or detect
where you are making particular rules for yourself or are tying yourself
in knots with your thoughts. Furthermore you will then discover what
you prescribe yourself. At this point we would like to remind you of
the section 'One Inner Rule Chases the Next' (Chapter 2).

If you have discovered various rules you will realise that a rule as
such is not yet connected to an inner 'bad feeling'. It is only when the
rule is violated, be it in your imagination or reality, that fear or
immediate panic is triggered off. So if you, for example, give yourself

the instruction 'Don't blush!' and simultaneously remember that you blushed in your last four speeches, your awareness of the possibility of its happening again can trigger twinges of fear in you. Or if you put yourself under pressure 'to appear to be in control of the situation at all costs', the possibility at the same time exists that you will not give a composed impression at all. Otherwise there would hardly be a reason for your prescribing it for yourself.

From this it also becomes clear that every positive instruction ('I must appear in control!', 'I must be perfect', 'I must get noticed!', 'They have to listen to me!') simultaneously includes its negation. Because if I have to be in control, it cannot be that I am not in control at the same time. It cannot be that I am not perfect or not noticeable or the others do not listen to me! So it becomes clear that evasive behaviour or a strategy for getting round a conflict lie even behind positively formulated rules: namely trying to avoid what is bad.

To begin with we will now introduce you to the method of 'focusing'. Various exercises enable you to get to know the particular way and the preconditions of the internal perception of focusing. Afterwards you will find experiments, exercises and instructions that build upon one another, helping you discover your fear and enabling its subsequent dissolution.

Focusing: Following your Internal Voice

Focusing is a method of encountering yourself with a loving acceptance. It shows how you can face and welcome your own feelings of fear, grief, anger and happiness as they surface. To relate to one's feelings, to be conscious in general of one's own feelings, or to control the flow of feelings already by themselves enrich many of our workshop participants. They often feel it is a rediscovery and relearning of a lost relationship with themselves. Focusing describes how we can learn and cultivate the ability to get in touch with ourselves. Not just to stir up feelings or to confront them, but to understand them better is the actual goal. Focusing, as a method of breaking down the fear of speaking, involves perceiving and exploring feelings in order to understand them better. This enables us to abandon rules that prevent us from perceiving ourselves and sometimes even our entire life circumstances as they are. Often enough we look through a pair of glasses which we would not have prescribed for ourselves. When we take them off we mostly find that we are able to act more freely and resolutely.

The philosopher and psychotherapist Eugene Gendlin is the founder of Focusing. At the beginning of the Sixties he conducted research at the University of Chicago on the effectiveness of various therapies. The scientific discovery he made was that successful therapy was guaranteed neither by the way the therapy was conducted nor by the abilities of the individual therapist alone. He found that the ability of clients to get in touch with their own feelings, inner images and sentiments plays just as important, if not more important a role. Focusing was a result of this research. Its aim is to teach you to get in touch with your own experiences.

Focusing helps you to understand your feelings better, to clarify problems and to make decisions. You are probably familiar with the feeling of having discussed a problem over and over again with your family or friends. It only reassures and affords relief for the moment, but the fact that a friend or somebody who is close to you is prepared really to listen to you makes a difference. And that's worth a lot! But in reality your problem, your feeling or your indecision has not changed. In your mind you have trodden the same path over and over again. Your insight probably does not exceed what you already knew in the first place. If you try focusing you can experience overcoming the tendency to tie yourself in mental knots or feeling that you have come to a dead end. With Focusing you find a new way of approaching your problems and finding solutions that may at times surprise you.

The central point of Focusing is not to think the problem through from all perspectives as usual and to go over it again and again, but to stop for a moment and take the time to turn your attention inwards into your body. If you allow yourself this peace, you will experience an at first only vague and indescribable feeling about the problem or the thing to which you give your attention in this particular way. Frequently this feeling is at first felt as a vague sensation (for example, as a pulling, pressing, trembling, queasiness or something similar) in your stomach or chest area. Gendlin calls this often still unspecific sensory perception or quality which is sensed or internally visible in relationship to your problem 'felt-sense'.

You can direct questions at this vague sensory perception, to the 'felt-sense', for example: 'How does this "trembling" feel? 'Where do I feel this "pressure" the most?', 'What is it that makes me feel so queasy about this matter?' and so on. With a little patience words, pictures or memories emerge from this first 'resonance' that relate to your problem or subject. It takes time – perhaps a few minutes – for you to name this inner sensory perception without falling back on the familiar and frequently pre-prepared thoughts that you know by rote, and thereby hitting the usual dead end again.

In this way frequently unknown or repressed aspects or qualities of the particular problem show themselves – or we consciously experience feelings that we usually evade. Gendlin once said 'Focusing is a small door.' If we go through this door we step into an inner realm of experience that frequently itself opens up new experiences and discoveries.

Before we continue explaining the method, we would at this point like to offer you your first opportunity of trying out Focusing practically. In the following exercise we have chosen a subject that is not related to your fear of speaking. First of all it is about having an experience with your 'felt-sense'. You can experience the difference between, on the one hand, merely pondering over something and, on the other, attempting to relate to it by focusing.

We recommend that you read through the whole text first. Then you can take a section at a time. Another possibility is to record the instructions on tape, bearing in mind that you should speak slowly and make pauses. A further suggestion is to conduct this exercise with a friend who reads the instructions to you at your pace. Try out the methods and see which one is the most appropriate for you for getting to know Focusing and dismantling your fear.

'The Birthday Exercise'

– You should set aside approximately 15 minutes for this exercise.

– Start by making yourself as comfortable as possible, perhaps in your favourite easy chair, and find some peace by just closing your eyes and focusing on your breathing. Let the thoughts that are going through your head move on like little white clouds, and focus on your breathing.

– Where can you feel your breathing? Perhaps you will notice how the air streams in and out of your nose and how your abdominal wall rises and sinks. Let yourself become conscious of how you breathe in and out without influencing it. Remain focused on the rhythm and flow of your breathing.

Once you feel more calm and relaxed take two deep breaths and turn to our little focusing exercise.

– Try to relate to the following situation on an inner level: Imagine it is your birthday today. Allow pictures, memories, noises, feelings or physical sensations to surface that you associate with 'having a birthday'. Be conscious of what unfolds inside of you. Take the necessary time to turn your attention inwards, to listen to, to feel, to concentrate on to your abdomen and chest. Wait for a feeling to arise – maybe only a vague one at first – that describes 'having a birthday' as a whole. Ask yourself: 'What does having a birthday feel like to me? What does the mood it puts me in feel like?'

- Take your time to feel this inner atmosphere.

- If you wait patiently and do not force yourself to do anything, eventually a picture or words may emerge that correspond to the vague sensory perception.

- On a physical level you can sense whether what you have found is apt if your whole body (not only your mind) says 'yes': 'Yes this is what it feels like to have a birthday.'

- You may find that you have found something on the subject of birthdays that you did not expect, something that amazes or confuses you. Try to accept and welcome this new aspect that you have just discovered. Tell yourself: 'This is the way it is.'

- To conclude this little experiment direct your attention once more to your breathing and focus on this for a while.

- Sense your body again, how you are sitting or lying.

- Take as much time as you want to open your eyes and gradually make the transition from inner to outer sensory perception.

Having conducted this experiment you may have noticed the difference between focusing and analysis. Let us now take it a step further.

The conscious experiencing of feelings is made possible through Focusing. At the same time you decide how much you want to experience and how much you want to discover by directing and sharpening your inner attention towards your subject.

We would now like to show you how you can apply Focusing purposefully to dismantle the inner rules that block you or cause you stress. So how can I stop making rules for myself on an inner level? The answer is: by ceasing to push away or avoid perceiving unpleasant feelings or sides of myself that I do not like.

You can do this by consciously focusing on your inner feelings, pictures and sensory perceptions which may be related to the violation of your rules.

You can teach yourself this special art of perception. However, before we go into more detail and describe the conditions and preconditions for this, we would like quickly to summarise the focusing process.

Inner rule	*Focusing*
'I am not allowed to blush!'	Perceive on an inner level feelings, images, thoughts etc. that are related to blushing.
'I must be perfect!'	On an inner level, face up to the possibility of 'not being perfect', feel your way into how it is not to be perfect.
'I must be loved!'	Become conscious of the feelings, pictures etc. which are associated with the idea of not being loved.

A case study –
what it is that makes Claire scared when she is speaking

Claire, a student, was very scared of speaking, unprepared, in front of a group of people that she did not know. Over the last few months she had on several occasions tried to avoid exposing herself to this kind of situation in the first place. At the same time she noticed that the unpleasant feeling that she experienced at first exacerbated itself more and more until it escalated to an inner panic. The very thought of having to stand in front of a group and speak caused her heart to start racing. Claire wanted to get out of this vicious circle and decided to explore her fear. She sat down on her sofa, relaxed and allowed herself to spend half an hour focusing. She closed her eyes and let an inner speech situation that she had experienced a week ago take shape before her inner eye.

She could picture the situation clearly: everyday life at university, overcrowded lecture room, you can cut the air with a knife. A paper is being presented. Her temper is rising, she disagrees with the speaker, has counter-arguments. The discussion begins. She wants to raise her hand, voice her objections, ask her questions. Whilst the others are disputing she gasps for air twice, makes another attempt, but her throat feels constricted. She gives up. Then another student addresses the very aspect that she wanted to. The contribution is taken up with interest, reaffirmed by many people and provides a constructive turning-point in the discussion. She herself sits slumped in her chair, her fear turned to anger, anger at not having been able to open her mouth.

Claire wanted to get to the bottom of her fear of speaking and in her imagination she took herself back to the moment when her fear was the greatest: when she breathed in deeply and her throat felt constricted. She paused the film of her memory before her inner eye at this point and concentrated on the unpleasant feeling. It was as if a thick lump were in her throat. She could sense the colourful, clever and daring thoughts dancing around her abdomen like sparkling wine and a fat cork sitting in her throat that refused to let anything out. In continuing her focusing session she closely examined the cork, felt and listened to it. It sat firmly in her throat, as if saying 'Just don't let anything out!' When Claire became conscious of this, the pressure in her throat eased a little. She had become inquisitive and wanted to find out more about her fear. On an inner level she asked herself: 'What would be bad about letting something out?' and she imagined she had given her opinion, had expressed her criticism. This image was accompanied by an unpleasant feeling that formed an image: she pictured the other students laughing at her, pointing fingers at her, and it was as if she was shrivelling up. She felt like a shrinking, deflating balloon; she felt herself getting smaller and smaller. Then an old memory she had almost forgotten came into her mind. She saw herself as a small girl, standing in front of the class, and everybody was laughing at her because she suddenly no longer knew how to carry on speaking. Claire became vividly conscious of the old feeling. She identified the core of her fear in this feeling she had always tried to avoid. She greeted this sensitive part of her soul, let it in and imagined sitting down beside it. When she asked the little frightened girl what she might need, she saw the inner response: 'Stand by me, protect me.' She imagined that she was doing this, took hold of her arm and told the laughing children: 'Stop laughing, everybody gets stuck sometimes!' She dwelt on this experience for two minutes, five minutes, and became conscious of how the unpleasantness slowly started to ease off. Claire decided to leave the process at this point and to come back to this old wound later, when she would give it renewed attention.

The purpose of this example was to give you an impression of the way in which a process of inner sensory perception can take its course. In the following we would like to offer additional information that will further clarify this method. To begin with, we will in a summary describe the various phases of the focusing process for deconstructing inner rules and will comment on them by using the case study.

Out of the Strait Jacket: Focusing that Puts you at Ease

Step I   *Looking at the stage set*

In this phase the aim is to develop as lively an image as possible of the problematic situation and to introduce it vividly to your mind's eye. In what kind of situations do I encounter my fear? What do I find difficult?
In the example: for Claire it is the situation of speaking in front of big groups when she is unprepared, and she imagines an everyday situation at university.

Step II   *Discovering the rules*

Here it is a matter of going in search of one or all of the inner rules that are activated in this kind of problematic situation. How do I put myself under pressure? What is not allowed to happen?
In the example: Claire discovers the rule 'I must not let anything out!' is stuck in her throat like a cork.

Step III   *Violating the rule*

In this phase imagine that the preceding rule you just discovered is violated, in other words, that exactly what is not allowed to happen, happens.
In the example: Claire imagines voicing her opinions and criticisms, that is, 'letting something out'.

Step IV   *Perceiving the 'bad-feeling'*

Ask yourself what would be bad about this. In asking about the bad, the unpleasant aspects of the situation, you are, in this phase, getting in touch with the feelings, images and emotions that have been pushed away on an inner level by relevant rule.
In the example: on questioning the bad aspects Claire suddenly imagines being laughed at by the students in her seminar.

Step V   *Unfurling and pondering*

The images, physical sensations and feelings that are associated with the bad aspects unfurl. You look at them, listen and feel into them. In the process they may develop or change.

In the example: Claire shrivels up more and more as she imagines being laughed at by the others. She has the picture of a deflating balloon in her mind. Suddenly she remembers her traumatic school experience of being laughed at by her fellow pupils.

Step VI   *Healing the wound*

In this phase you sense, listen to and eavesdrop tenderly on the core of the bad aspects. What is the central issue for me in this situation? What is the core of what is bad? What would this bruised, anxious or helpless side of me need? What would provide some light, strength or help? Listen for answers that come from inside you and sense what it is that changes. Let a picture or word emerge from your experience and ponder on it for a while.

In the example: Claire again experiences the unpleasant feelings she once had and recognises the feeling of being alone and exposed as the core of her fear. She comes face to face with the inner wounded girl and hears what she needs.

The described steps are not so easy to separate out in an actual focusing session. Sometimes the session is interrupted because it is no longer possible on an inner level to concentrate on the unpleasant and on the problematic. If you experience this when you try focusing you can decide either to stop or to take a step back and start afresh from the point at which you felt you were in good contact with your subject on an inner level.

The central question of Focusing is: 'What is bad about this thing, about this feeling?' Try not to construct the answer in your head, but perceive the unpleasant, the core of what is bad on an inner level. This question supports the process of ceasing to make rules for yourself. If, for example, your rule is 'I'm not allowed to fail', the question would be: 'What is bad about my failing?' On an inner level you would for a moment stop prescribing this rule for yourself so that you can become conscious of what it would be like to fail. You would give attention to the associated images, feelings and sensations. This means the inner pressure and the tension can begin to dissolve.

In order to allow for complete awareness on an inner level, it will be helpful to you if you take into consideration the following preconditions, which may be understood as internal and external aids.

THE SUPPORTIVE INNER CLIMATE –
AND HOW YOU CAN CREATE IT

If you decide to practise Focusing, it makes sense to heed the following four preconditions important for the inner perception process:

• making space

• inner attentiveness

• open inquisitiveness

• correct distance

In order to turn your thoughts inwards you need a quiet room where you will not be disturbed, sufficient time and good conditions. You can discover below how to create these for yourself and why there might be reasons for your focusing's 'not working out'.

Before You Start – Making Space for Yourself

Making space means creating good conditions, internal and external in order to be able to turn your attention inwards so that you can concern yourself with the fear of speaking.

You can try focusing anywhere where you can remain undisturbed for a while and feel comfortable. Note the following factors:

– Can you ensure that you are not going to be disturbed? (For example door closed, telephone turned off, 'please do not disturb' sign etc.)

– Are there sounds or noises that disturb you? Can you get rid of these disturbances or improve the situation? (If you cannot, it sometimes helps to listen to these noises. Imagine they are a symphony and that during the performance you turn down the volume slowly and redirect your attention inwards towards your body and listen to your heartbeat or breathing.)

– Does the temperature suit you? Can you regulate it if necessary? Do you need a blanket? Do you want to sit or lie down? Can you somehow make yourself more comfortable?

In order to start focusing it is beneficial to get rid of possible disturbances. Give particular and lengthy attention to what cannot be changed, as described above in the case of interfering noises. In spite of these good preparations it is of course possible that you notice that something is distracting you in the course of the focusing process. For example, you might start to feel a chill or your posture might become uncomfortable. Make sure that you rearrange yourself so that you feel comfortable again and can dedicate yourself to your subject.

When you have created the best possible external space, you can, if necessary, start creating your inner space. Internally you can also create good conditions – in effect a good atmosphere – to practise Focusing. In your imagination this is like an inner sorting out; you can compare it to clearing up an old junk room where lots of things have collected, putting things on shelves and throwing away old rubbish.

You can create inner space by asking yourself:

– Do I have any physical tensions or pains that demand my attention?

– If these tensions or pains cannot be remedied by external changes, for example, of posture, give these sensations your attention by consciously breathing towards the point of tension or if it is possible, put your hand in that position for support.

– Are there any circular thoughts that I am unable to let go of at the moment?

– Especially at the beginning of the process it can be difficult to relate to the subject. Perhaps things are going through your mind that you have just been dealing with, or you still have to deal with. Be aware of these thoughts but do not hang on to them or start to grapple with them. Let them go past you internally. Sometimes picturing things helps: imagine you are standing on a bridge beneath which a river is flowing. Leaves float on the river. Let your thoughts drift past you like the leaves or concentrate on little clouds that drift past in the sky.

– It can be more difficult dealing with problematic thoughts or feelings that are of importance to you and of which you become conscious when you have settled down in the described way. There are two possibilities that are open to you. You can decide to occupy yourself with these first, or you can try to create a good distance by setting these subjects aside for the moment. You can do this in your imagination by picturing the following: as they emerge, put the problems or thoughts and feelings that do not directly have anything to do with you fear of speaking into individual packages, sacks, safes or something similar. You can then tie up the 'packages' and in your imagination place them right at the back of a shelf in the cellar or put them in front of the door in order to get rid of them for the time being. Stash away these 'packaged problems' knowing that they are not going to run away and that you can turn to them at a later point.

If you find it difficult to put to one side the subjects that crop up in your imagination, some people find it helps to jot them down quickly: a call that needs to be made, a conversation with a neighbour or a list of errands. Then you have it in black and white, it cannot vanish from your mind and you create inner space for yourself again.

If you find that your thoughts digress during the focusing process or get in the way and that they are not directly related to the subject you are dealing with, treat them in the way just described and return to your subject of focusing.

Inner Attentiveness

If the outer and inner spaces are right, you can turn to your inner experiences. In focusing you deal with a problem differently from the way that you would normally. You do not think it through, analyse its causes, explore any connections, but imagine the problem and perceive what you feel. This takes time because answers do not come as quickly from the body as they do from the mind. Wait, ask yourself the question 'How is the whole problem for me?' and be inwardly attentive.

Being inwardly attentive involves turning your attention inwards via your senses, towards your inner space of experience: to look inside, to sense inside, to listen, to feel, to taste, and so on. This approach may at first seem strange, especially since you are not used to the idea of experiencing your body as a space that reacts to external events or questions with images, sensations and feelings. We will provide you with an exercise after this description that will enable you to experience this.

Turning your attention inwards so that you perceive your inner experiences is a simple activity that you do not need to learn, but can rediscover. Children have a natural ability to perceive their inner world when they are playing or painting and to express it in a lively way. As adults we forget this to such an extent that we try to control our feelings towards others and ourselves. Being inwardly attentive means perceiving what is, as it is.

Forget the 'Watch out!' attitude or excessively anxious attentiveness. Forget probing searches or inner judgements. Be nice and loving towards yourself. Perceive what is. And if at first there is nothing, then feel your way into this inner nothingness. And if you find a lot, embrace what you find with open arms and say: 'Ah, I see, there's quite a lot going on inside me.'

Open Inquisitiveness

A Focusing session will take its own course, one that cannot be predicted or ascertained. Fixation on results or proceeding purposefully with inquisitorial rigour will not bring about the relevant type of perception. Focusing assumes the preparedness to tread an untrodden path, not one that is pre-determined in your mind. Focusing is a letting happen, and requires patience, inquisitiveness and trust. Maybe you will notice that during the focusing process thoughts worm their way in, for instance:

- 'What boring images!' or

- 'I'm not experiencing anything, I'm imagining the situation and yet nothing is happening!' or

- 'That should surely feel really bad, yet I only feel a slight pulling sensation in my abdomen ...'

Then you have left the attitude of 'open inquisitiveness' and have begun to evaluate, to put yourself under pressure and to prescribe new rules. These thoughts interfere with the process of perception because they seek to change what is.

At such moments it is helpful to be conscious of your thoughts, to listen to them and realise: 'Aha, now I'm getting impatient', so that you can open yourself again to what is. If you understand that you are putting yourself under pressure to produce something special, it may also be a relief to start the focusing process with the following attitude: 'I don't have to do anything! I can sense how it feels not to have to do anything: not to have to arrive at anything, not to have to find anything out, not to have to achieve anything. I don't have to do anything now! I can sense how the good feeling of not having to do anything is spreading within me and I notice that I am, at the same time, open to and inquisitive about what might reveal itself.'

We invite you to try the following exercise for the attitudes of both 'inner attentiveness' and 'open inquisitiveness', which are concerned with getting to know and perceive your body as space of experience. Incidentally this exercise is a good aid to relaxing and forever produces new sensations and images.

Again we recommend that you record the instructions for the exercise on tape. Make enough pauses in the recording so that you have enough time later on during your process. The questions in the instructions are intended as an aid to developing your inner experiences and your perception rather than a challenge to answer them with precision.

Exercise: 'Sensing Body Space'

– On an inner level relax. Allow yourself approximately 30 minutes for this experiment. Make yourself comfortable either sitting or lying down and sense whether you have found a good body posture. Then become aware of your breathing for 1–2 minutes.

– Now find out whether you can sense your breathing in the area of your stomach region. By way of support you can rest your hands on your stomach and imagine that you are breathing towards your hands. You can feel your abdominal wall rising and sinking.

– Every time you breathe out, direct your attention a little more towards your stomach area. It might help if you imagine climbing down towards it step by step.

– Perceive your stomach area as a space. What does it feel like there? What does it look like there? Is there a place in your stomach area that feels particularly pleasant or unpleasant? What is it like there on the whole? Are there pictures, feelings or maybe colours that are created here? Let yourself be led by your perception and allow yourself a few minutes to do this.

– Now say goodbye to your stomach area, concentrate on your breathing again and breathe in your chest area. Put your hands on your chest and be conscious of how your hands rise and sink slightly. Turn your attention towards this area of your body. What is it like here? What does it feel like? What does it look like here? Be inquisitive about exploring this area too. Take time to discover it.

– Now turn your attention to your neck and try and experience your neck on the inside as a space. Can you sense your breath coursing through your neck? Perhaps you can imagine breathing in your neck. Also take a look around here, sense what it feels like or listen out for what you can hear. What is it like in your neck? Are there feelings, colours or sounds?

- Finish this exercise by being conscious of your breathing and by sensing for a moment your body as a whole. Sense how you are sitting or lying. Now you can slowly turn your attention outwards. Take your time. Start by listening for noises, perhaps also become conscious of the smell of the room, and then slowly open your eyes and look around again and get your orientation back.

We hope you were able to experience the two basic attitudes of 'inner attentiveness' and 'open inquisitiveness' in this exercise. You may have been able to experience your body as a space and have discovered feelings, images, sounds and physical sensations that you had not previously intended to perceive.

The third basic attitude we are now going to describe probably arose automatically when you did the previous exercise. It is usually more significant when dealing with problematic subjects in focusing sessions.

Maintaining Correct Distance

Here we are concerned with maintaining the correct inner distance between yourself and your problem. Focusing aims to achieve neither an immersion in your problem, a wallowing in your feelings, nor abstract theoretical philosophising about it without inner emotional participation.

At this point we would like to suggest another simple experiment that sums up the main principle of this attitude.

Exercise: 'Correct Distance'

Examine the palms of your hands. Direct your attention toward the folds and lines that make your hand a unique structure. You will automatically choose the correct distance required for you to focus clearly. You will not hold your hand directly in front of your eyes just as you will not stretch your arm out as far as possible to look at it (unless of course you are long-sighted). There is a distance between your eye and your hand that seems exactly right.

This applies to Focusing in exactly the same way when it comes to the distance between you as perceiver and your inner experience. In order to be able to perceive in a casual manner and establish a relationship with your sentiments and feelings, the correct distance is required. You will have already have found this on occasions when you have not felt as if the problem inside you was part of your being, yet still felt as if you were the observer of something that affected you from inside.

What can you do if you lose the correct distance, or if your feelings during the focusing process threaten to be too unpleasant, too difficult or too emotional?

Firstly: you can bring the process to an end. You are in a position to open your eyes and stop at any time. You are neither hypnotised nor in a trance, but in a relaxed state, so you are always mistress of yourself and you can act self-determinedly.

Secondly: you can stay with your perceptions and use various images to help re-establish the correct distance between yourself and your inner experiences. Here are a couple of examples of how this works in practice:

> During a focusing session, a seminar participant had the feeling that she was being crushed by a ball that was sitting on her breastbone and getting bigger and bigger. She re-established the distance by imagining that she was breathing through the ball. So she was able to continue perceiving the ball and exploring it further.

> Another participant was scared of confronting a fear that seemed to look like a gigantic monster. In her imagination she put the monster in a boat and let it drift out to sea until she felt herself at a safe distance on the beach. From this distance she was able to take a more precise look at her fear and slowly bring it ever closer towards her.

In dismantling inner rules we often encounter unpleasant feelings or old wounds. To let these sensations be has a healing effect. Old wounds need air and light. If, however, the sensations become too severe, so that it no longer seems possible for you to dwell on them attentively, use your imagination: establish some distance between yourself and these sensations. Take three steps back and imagine that you are on a raised stand or wrap yourself in protective coat and welcome the feelings by telling them that you can see how big they are.

The preconditions described above are intended to help the focusing process run smoothly. If Focusing does not work for you, you could ask yourself:

– Am I really being inwardly attentive or is there something in the foreground that is disturbing me, for example, time pressure, noise and so on?

- Can I inquisitively and openly observe my experiences or do I already know what they are about anyway? Am I avoiding the central points?

- Have I got the correct distance between what I want to observe in focusing or do I feel devoured by my problem or too far away, so far in fact that I am unable to observe it any longer?

If you would like to read up in greater detail on the method of focusing we recommend that you take a look at a book by Ann Weiser-Cornell called *The Power of Focusing: A Practical Guide to Emotional Self-Healing*, which discusses focusing as a self-help method and offers a lot of practical exercises.

So far we have explained the essence and the process of focusing to you. You were able to have your first experiences of it by using the exercises given. In the following section we are going to apply Focusing directly to the breaking-down of the fear of speaking.

LOOKING FEAR IN THE FACE: OR HOW RULES DISINTEGRATE

As already discussed, the aim of Focusing is to break up inner rules, and thereby to pay attention to feelings, thoughts, images and physical sensations that we usually try to avoid by laying down inner rules. We will now recommend some exercises that will assist your perception and that you can use for your own self-help. We will complement and explain these exercises with descriptions of experiences and case examples from our own coaching sessions. Maybe you will be able to identify with one or other of these examples – but it may also show you what a diverse range of feelings, images and sensations can be associated with the phenomenon of the 'fear of speaking'.

With 'Chattering Teeth and Trembling Knees' – Physical Symptoms of Fear

Exercise: 'Feeling the Fear'

Once again take yourself back to a difficult speech situation which scares you. As you did in the exercise 'thought out loud' ensure that you take sufficient time to project yourself in person into the situation. Do not concentrate on your thoughts but be conscious of how the fear becomes perceptible in you. Can you feel the fear physically? How does your body react in situations of fear? Note down the symptoms of your fear.

Fear of speaking in public can be revealed in your whole body. Who does not know what it is like to experience the feeling of 'your heart sinking into your knees'. The physical symptoms of the women coached by us ranged from a slightly accelerated heartbeat to dizziness and faintness.

Here is an overview of possible *symptoms of fear from head to toe*:

Headache, blushing, red blotches, blackout, tears in your eyes, 'cotton wool in your head', dry mouth, salivation, dizziness, impairment of perception, sweating, hot flushes, lump in your throat, quivering voice, choking, breathlessness, pressure on your chest, pounding heart, disturbance of heartbeat, stabbing pain in the thorax, pain in the stomach, nausea, cramp, diarrhoea, pressure on the bladder, shaking or clammy hands, trembling knees, shaky legs, tension in your legs.

Physical symptoms of fear are frequently perceived as threats, which may lead to an intensification of the feeling of fear: 'God help us! My heart is suddenly beating so fast – THAT MUST NOT HAPPEN!'... and then it begins to beat even faster. The experience of fear itself becomes a catastrophe that simply must be avoided: what arises is the fear of fear. This vicious circle of bodily reactions is increased by the fear of fear; it means that a person has to observe herself in order stay 'in control', so that a person's thoughts mainly revolve around avoiding these physical symptoms of fear. We have named this critical self-observation the *Lenor Effect* (borrowing from the Seventies advert in which, on expressing guilt, a housewife is duplicated). Those people affected by it experience it as an internal division, one experiencing and one that observes the experiencing and would like to extinguish it. Your concentration is for the most part directed towards trying to get rid of perceiving the symptoms of fear. It is similar to the ticking clock that you find disturbing when trying to get to sleep. The more you concentrate on it, the louder it seems to become. The situation is just the same as far as your physical reactions are concerned: your heartbeat becomes unbearably loud, your face as red as a lobster, your knees tremble even more. A teacher who was perfectly capable of speaking without fear in front of a class, but regularly lost her nerve completely when in charge of parent evenings, described this condition as follows: 'It's as if I'm sitting in on myself. I stand next to myself, have a go at myself, hear myself speak and grow more and more nervous.'

Your concentration is absorbed by this 'inner crisis' and is barely available for what you have to say. It is not rare for this in turn to lead to the described blackout. The following comments made by a student describe the *Lenor Effect* vividly:

My head spins, my body feels drained of all blood, as if it weren't capable of doing anything anymore, as if it didn't belong to me anymore. My thoughts go round and round, but I can't form a single clear thought, everything is mixed up. My eyes can no longer see properly. They see everything but nothing, as if they have turned inwards, where they can see the mental knots I'm tying myself up in and look at them disparagingly. They are always watching me. There is complete chaos, a merry-go-round of thoughts.

This self-observation or standing-next-to-oneself is a clear signal that this woman is prescribing rules for herself that affect her behaviour: the eyes turn inwards and shake their head about the inner chaos: 'THAT MUST NOT HAPPEN!'

This psychological process is often similar to authoritarian, early childhood educational experiences: self-reproach, dressing downs, internal homilies on the one hand; fears, feelings of helplessness, powerlessness and inferiority on the other, as if there were two people inside fighting each other. And this inner battle is usually between our 'inner child' and an over-critical parent or a strict teacher, who interferes and tells us what we can and cannot do: 'Don't make such a fuss, stop shaking.' But the resistance of the 'child' follows the pressure of the 'parent's critical voice': it blocks or reacts with fear. Just as a child is not to be convinced with the words 'You don't need to be scared' we can give ourselves the order that we are not allowed to feel any fear. The way out of this inner crisis is to become aware of and accept our own fear, to behave benevolently and with friendliness towards it.

We recommend another exercise at this point. In order get closer to your fear in a different manner from usual, that is, via thoughts and language, we are going to give you the instructions with which you can attempt to perceive your fear physically and then paint it. You will need a large piece of paper (A2 or at least two pieces of A4 stuck together) and wax crayons. This is not about producing an artistic painting. After you have felt the fear in your body try and find a means of expressing it: strokes, shapes, colours, something abstract, or concrete inner images.

Exercise: 'Painting Fear'

- Find a place where you are not going to be disturbed and are comfortable and can draw for half an hour.

- First lean back, draw deep breaths and give yourself a little break to reflect. If you feel like it, close your eyes.

- Take the time to prepare yourself on an inner level and get in touch with your fear.

- When you feel ready, again search for an image of a situation in which you had to speak that you found unpleasant. Let the situation run like an internal film. Stop the film at the point you find most unpleasant and frightening. Be conscious of how your body adapts. How does your fear feel physically? Maybe there is a particular area of your body where you sense what you fear most. Do not expend any effort, but wait until something comes about of its own accord.

- Alter your inner consciousness so that you are now seeing rather than primarily feeling. What does it look like inside you? Is there an inner picture, shape or colours? Observe what the fear looks like inside you. What kind of atmosphere does this image bring with it? Be conscious of everything that unfolds. Give yourself time and hold on to the image inside.

- If you examine this picture as a whole, do you find that it has a core, something that is central for you? Is there a word or a sentence for it? What would you call it? What title would it have?

- Now take a step back from the image and move from your inner perception, from looking inwards, gradually outwards. Be conscious of how you breathe, how you are sitting, and find your bearings again in the room.

- When you feel ready, take your coloured pencils and paper and draw your fear.

If you now have in your hands a picture of your feeling of fear, you may experience that an expression for it has emerged, which you previously would not have been able to name or describe in this way. This expression is a further step towards your fear, a step towards perceiving and taking it seriously, just as it has revealed itself to you, without judging yourself.

The main purpose of the following exercise is to sharpen your perception on a physical level.

Exercise: 'Welcoming Bodily Sensations'

– Direct your attention to your body. What can you perceive there? Try to observe your bodily sensations, without evaluating or influencing them. Say 'hello' to your sensations: 'Now I notice how I breathe, in and out, hello, breath!', 'Now my shoulder is tensing up, hello tenseness!', 'Now I can feel my heart beating, hello, heartbeat!', 'Now I can feel my cold feet. Hello, cold feet!' and so on. Feel inside yourself, from your toes to your head. What are you perceiving right now?

If you are in a relaxed state this exercise is relatively easy to conduct. Try also to perceive, consciously without evaluating your body, unpleasant situations that make you feel agitated, scared or angry inside. By doing this you will also learn to perceive your bodily reactions as they are in moments of tension and will not classify them as being additional sources of fear. Just as you are probably able to accept your heart's pounding when you are 'head over heels' in love without evaluating it negatively, you will also, after a while, be able to encounter your heart pounding when you are speaking with something like these words: 'Ah, I am worked up and my heart is pounding, hello, pounding heart.'

To summarise:

1. Bodily symptoms reveal themselves from head to toe.

2. Bodily symptoms sometimes trigger off fear themselves ('Fear of fear').

3. Most of the time bodily symptoms cannot be controlled at will (for example: 'I must not blush now').

4. The attempt to control body symptoms usually leads to an intensification of them ...

5. ... and frequently to the *Lenor Effect.*

   Aim: To reduce physical symptoms by becoming conscious of your sensations as they are without evaluating them or pushing them away.

In the same way that you have just perceived your physical symptoms of fear, we would like to encourage you to relax your rules and break down your speech inhibitions in the next part of this section.

Stop Making Rules for Yourself

As previously, you can record the following focusing instructions on tape. Again we recommend that you leave enough pauses during speech so that later on you will have sufficient time and will not feel hassled. Moreover the longer you take for your perception exercise the more it will enable you to develop your experience and stop making rules for yourself. Depending on how deep the rules are ingrained, it will require different amounts of attention until you can feel a change setting in. You may have to carry out several focusing processes until you feel more at ease and relieved on an inner level. Do not force yourself to stay with your sensations, feelings and images or thoughts if they become too unpleasant for you. It is better to decide to come back to them at a later time.

You could also get a close friend to read these instructions to you. This exercise takes at least 30 minutes. The questions in the instructions are once again intended as an aid to unfolding and perceiving the sensations and pictures of your inner experience, and are not meant to stir up thoughts.

Exercise: Focusing to Put Yourself at Ease

- To begin, create an outer framework and inner space.

- Direct your attention from outwards to inwards.

- If you feel like it close your eyes.

- Follow your breathing. Every time you breath out travel further into yourself.

Step I   *Looking at the Stage Set*

When you feel ready inside, get into contact with an unpleasant situation in which you are required to speak, for example, one that you have already experienced, or one that lies ahead of you. Let this situation come to life before your mind's eye.

- What is this situation like?
- What do you see with your mind's eye?
- What can you hear?
- What thoughts are going through your head?
- How do you feel in this situation?

Step II   *Discovering the Rules*

- Make sure you are aware of the thoughts that put inner pressure on yourself.
- Do you make rules for yourself on how you or those listening should be inside? Or is there anything that is not allowed to happen under any circumstances in this situation?
- If you have found rules that put you under pressure, ask yourself once more: 'What puts me under the most pressure, what is the central thing?'

Step III   *Violating the Rule*

Once you have discovered a central rule, imagine the possibility of violating it. Imagine that what is not allowed to happen under any circumstances does happen. Take your time to picture this.

Pause

- Look this possibility in the face. How does this make you feel? What does this image trigger inside you?

Pause

Step IV   *Perceiving the 'Bad Feeling'*

– Now ask yourself: 'What is bad/unpleasant about it?' Investigate what is bad and let the answer to this question emerge, as if from the inside.

Pause

Step V   *Unfurling and Pondering*

- Direct your attention towards your stomach and chest area, and watch, sense, listen to what unfurls there.
- What is 'the bad' like? Is there a place in your body, where you can sense it in particular? Does a feeling emerge with the bad? Maybe an image or colour emerges that matches it?
- Perceive what reveals itself as it is and develops, however little or much it may be doing so at this moment. Even if it is unpleasant, stay with perceiving the bad and try accompanying your experience like a loving friend.

Step VI   *Healing the Wound*

- Are you conscious of a centre, a core of what is bad? What is central? Stay with your experiencing of the bad in order to answer this question.
- Can you give a name to this central thing, describe or express it? Is there a sentence, word, image or movement that matches this sensation?
- When you have got in touch with the core of what is bad, direct the following question at it: 'What would it take to make it feel better there?' – 'What would help?' or 'What would be a good step to take?' And wait and see whether an answer comes from inside. Sense what changes in the process come about.
- Ask yourself what is still missing in order to complete the process of awareness. Perhaps you would like to return to an important point or keep hold of an image or word inside, so that it does not get lost.
- Allow yourself time to do this.

Conclusion

- Slowly end this focusing process by consciously perceiving your breathing. With every breath you take, sense the surface on which you are lying or the chair on which you are sitting. With every breath you take come back into the room. Listen to the noises and slowly start blinking and then opening your eyes. If you feel like it, yawn or stretch.

- Before you continue reading or doing something else think about whether you had a new experience or made a new discovery or whether something old and familiar came back into your consciousness.

If you feel like it you can now look for a way of expressing what you have just experienced. This can be particularly helpful if you notice that you can sense the unpleasantness 'that you are still carrying it around with you', that it has not changed through focusing and you find it difficult to let go of it inside. If you have conducted the focusing process in the company of a close friend, you can talk about it – you may feel you want to write down the experience, or to express what you have seen inside in the form of a picture, reproducing shape and colour. What is important is not the way you do this, but the process of moving from sensing to expressing.

It is possible that a new, perhaps more deeply ingrained imperative reveals itself as the core of what is bad (Step VI) in the focusing process that you have just practised. You can explore this in the same way in another focusing round. It is also possible to repeat the focusing process several times, for example, by perceiving the same situation on an inner level anew the following day. During the process you can observe whether you experience similar 'bad feelings' or whether your experience of fear of speaking changes. Perhaps you hardly sense any unpleasant feelings any more at the thought of violating this rule. This could be a sign that you have stopped prescribing this rule for yourself. You have deleted the inner instruction. Experiment with this exercise and make yourself aware of how your experience changes.

Now look at these two practical exercises for two common rules: the fear of being the centre of attention and the fear of being rejected.

Exercise: 'Served up on a Plate'

Find yourself a comfortable seat and take your time getting in touch with yourself and relaxing. Imagine a speech situation where you are standing or sitting in front of an audience. It does not matter whether you have really experienced this situation or whether you make the whole thing up; the main thing is that you can, on an inner level, experience how all eyes are on you and that you are the centre of attention. Immerse yourself in this scene: you are standing in front of lots of people, everybody is looking at you and waiting for you to start speaking. Practise focusing as we have described to accompany the thoughts and feelings that are emerging.

Exercise: 'Rejected and Booed off the Stage'

Take your time and find a comfortable place where you can sit undisturbed. Let a situation in which you are speaking but are being distracted by those listening to you form in front of your mind's eye. Perhaps a speech situation of this kind lies ahead of you, in which case, let this future situation unfold in your imagination. Or you may have experienced this in reality, in which case, immerse yourself in the memory of the situation. Imagine that you and what you are saying is rejected by the people listening to you. What does the audience do? How do you recognise that you are being rejected? Stay with this idea of experiencing a 'flop' and possibly arousing protest. Let your feelings of unease or whatever other sensations develop take their course inside you.

With the aid of the focusing instructions, focus on what is unpleasant or 'awful' when you experience rejection by your audience.

In situations where you notice you are inclined to issue yourself a stern instruction, pause for a little while and do some 'flash focusing'.

Exercise: 'Flash Focusing'

If you find that you put yourself under pressure with a rule or by prohibiting yourself from doing something, ask yourself 'What would be so bad about the something happening that is not supposed to happen?' Let the answer to this question emerge from the feeling that is associated with this vision. 'What is it that I find so unpleasant – bad – dreadful about it?' Perceive what is bad for a moment.

We have had good experiences with 'Flash Focusing' in our everyday lives. I remember a seminar situation in which the video camera refused to function. All the seminar participants waited eagerly for their first video recordings, and yet nothing would work. To tell the truth, this was my vision of a nightmare, the worst thing that could possibly happen. 'It can't be true!', I heard myself saying. 'Oh God, it's got to work now!' – orders that increased my sense of panic and were all equally pointless. I decided to do some 'Flash Focusing'. I made myself aware of the embarrassing feeling of having to admit to the participants that the recording was going to fall through. I sensed my heart racing and my clammy hands and let them be as they were for a few moments. The unpleasant feeling gradually began to subside and I started to feel calmer. 'The camera is broken.' Full stop. This is how it was and not any other way. At this I was able to think constructively again, to think of other possibilities. Five minutes later, when I tried again, the camera worked. If I had not already reached the conclusion, I was now convinced: technical equipment also has a soul.

The effectiveness of 'Flash Focusing' is not always as spectacular as this, but in most cases, especially in situations where you experience stress, it helps. Try it.

The following is another exercise that you can try if you anticipate feeling fear or insecurity in an approaching situation and when what you would most like to do is 'chicken out' of it: 'A test of courage.'

I am sure you are familiar with tests of courage from your childhood. A person who is courageous is not one who is not scared of particular situations but one who sees situations through despite any fear. Step by step, stop trying to avoid difficult situations. Avoiding situations which give rise to fear causes chronic fear because the opportunity of collecting positive experiences is taken away from you.

In the development of fear, avoidance has a boomerang effect. It increases the fear of fear.

This exercise enables you to simulate a forthcoming speech situation in your imagination and acts as a mock treatment for trying out your new way of dealing with fear before the situation arises. If you are scared, feel uneasiness or have stage fright, draw these feelings into your consciousness of the situation by ceasing to push them away on an inner level.

Exercise: 'A Test of Courage'

- In your mind's eye picture the situation that gives rise to fear: 'How do you feel? What is going on inside you?' Be conscious of everything that is related to your fear.

- Now imagine that despite sensing your uneasiness and agitation you act, for example speak, without being handicapped by it. You are conscious of your fear, welcome it as a bodily sensation and speak, ask to speak, criticise, introduce yourself, and so on.

- Paint a picture of how it is going to be possible for you to do what you want to do accompanied by your fear. And notice how the symptoms of fear slowly lose their intensity whilst you are speaking.

Do this exercise a few times in your imagination and then start practising in real speech situations. Consciously approach your fear and perceive it.

These are enough exercises and experiments with which to get going. Try them out. Test out whether they are useful to you – and if you notice that you do not want to confront your fear on your own, do not shy away from seeking professional help. Sometimes all it takes is a close friend to support your self-help by simply being there and listening, for example, when you do a focusing exercise.

And if everything associated with Focusing just does not work, have a look at whether there are any Focusing seminars being held near you – or just forget everything up until now and simply stop trying to get rid of your fear through ignoring it, diversion, avoidance, trivialisation, and so on. Confront it when it shows itself, deal with it, get in touch with it, live it – and make use of your fear of speaking as a guide for your personal development.

In the following chapter we are going to describe some helpful techniques designed to make it easier for you to enter into speech situations and gain new experiences.

4 Winning People Over Self-Confidently: Aids, Tips and Techniques

Many women who are afraid of speaking arrange their lives and everyday existence in such a way that they hardly ever or never get themselves into situations where they have to speak in front of a group of people. For this reason they hardly gain any experience of what guarantees success and is appropriate and of what often hinders success when giving a speech and is inappropriate.

On the other hand, there are women who are only a little scared or not at all scared of speaking in front of an audience, yet still do not know how to speak successfully. In most cases there has simply been no previous occasion on which these women have had to give a speech. However, after their private or professional circumstances have changed and they now want to speak in front of an audience, they realise that they simply do not have the appropriate rhetorical know-how.

We would like to suggest to you techniques and tips that at least in part make up for a lack of practice and experience when it comes to speaking in front of a group. This rhetorical know-how is not, however, a substitute for breaking down the fear of speaking. For as long as you suffer from the fear of speaking, the danger exists of your treating the following tips and hints as a 'must', that is, of your turning them into a mental corset. Because you are scared of failure you may cling to rules and notes but the effect this has is, for example, to turn the tip 'Give examples that have factual content' into a new inner rule: 'I must give examples otherwise nobody will understand me!' You will greatly increase your fear of speaking if you turn the following rhetorical techniques into new inner rules.

At this point let us clearly state: you will not be able to reduce your fear of speaking through knowledge of rhetorical techniques. But this speech know-how can make you more self-confident if you have already dismantled your inner rules and reduced your fear of speaking.

RIGHT FROM THE START

In this section we offer you techniques and tips that can make it easier for you prepare to speak in front of a group. Careful planning can make you more self-confident, especially if you rehearse your speech and record it. Yet all your preparations and rehearsals are no guarantee of your speech's turning out the way you imagined it would. A speech in front of an audience is a complex communication situation. The course your speech takes may be influenced by many factors. Maybe a part of your speech has become obsolete because a previous speaker has already said some of the things that you wanted to say. Or, perhaps somebody has made an assertion that you would like to refute. Perhaps the atmosphere in the room is a serious one and you realise that the amusing examples that you have peppered your speech with are not actually appropriate. There are all sorts of things that could happen during your speech that could lead to your having to alter a part or even all of your speech. This is why you cannot consider yourself to have made a mistake if you end up giving a different speech from the one you had intended to give.

Nevertheless, careful planning in advance will be to your advantage. When you plan a speech, you sound out the subject of your speech, you set the boundaries, find appropriate words, arrange the order of your arguments or subsidiary points. This acts as a kind of security rope that you put around yourself as you would if you were going on a mountain climbing expedition. It gives you the freedom to take a few risks that you had not planned.

PREPARING A SPEECH OR PRESENTATION

How thorough the preparations for you speech are will depend on the occasion of your speech or presentation and your practical experience.

The important occasion: A situation in which you have to speak and upon which a crucial professional or business turning point rests will in general require more consideration and more thorough planning than, for example, a speech to be held on a social occasion such as the birthday of a colleague.

Practical experience: Skilled speakers often only prepare the contents of the crucial passages and improvise the opening and closing words. If on the other hand you do not have much practice it is sensible to formulate the opening words and your closing sentence.

The Layout of Your Script

Before you put together your notes for a speech think about whether you want to flesh out your speech word for word or whether it is more sensible to have notes that contain cue words. This decision will also depend on two factors.

On how important your speech is: The more important your words are in public, the more important it is that you formulate them with precision. Word-for-word notes are most sensible in this case.

On your preferred mode of speaking: You can of course give your speech without recourse to any notes at all. If for professional reasons you are confident in a particular area and are used to talking about it in front of others, your speech will probably turn out better 'off the cuff' than if you use notes.

Scripts that are Fleshed out Word for Word

If you are speaking in public, perhaps giving a business talk or a presentation, it is often important that you speak in a way that allows your main points to be quoted easily, since your words could end up appearing in a written report, perhaps in a professional journal. The same applies if your speech is of programmatic or guiding significance, for example an inaugural speech as the chairperson of a committee. In any case, whenever what you say could be put on the scales and weighed up by public opinion, it is sensible to flesh your speech out word for word or at least to flesh out the crucial passages.

It is an art to be able to make a speech or give a presentation without having your listeners fall asleep. At first it may appear easier just to read out a speech, but in practice the result may easily sound boring or unintelligible or both.

The reason for this is that we formulate our sentences differently when we write them down from when we are speaking. Written sentences are more stilted, complicated and less accessible than our spoken sentences. If this comparatively complicated written language is read out loud, it requires a lot of concentration on the part of the listeners. Because the speaker is concentrating on reading off the script word for word she hardly looks at the audience. On top of this the speaker often speaks too quickly or in a monotonous voice. The result is a forgettable speech.

And now for a few useful hints at how to flesh out a word-for-word script:

Write your speech in 'spoken language'. If you pre-formulate your speech sentence by sentence it is possible that you will write as you speak. Make sure that you use a simple sentence structure and avoid using complex, convoluted sentences.

Make sure the layout of the pages of your script is clear. Do not write too much on each page and leave a wide margin on either side of the pages. You can see the whole of the text more clearly if the lines on the paper are not too wide. A line width that is suitable for quickly skimming the text is for example that of newspapers and is approximately 25 to 30 letters long.

Make a note of your 'stage directions'. To guard against the danger of just rattling off your speech, you can simply make notes in your script on the way to speak. You can mark with a particular colour the parts of the texts where you want to speak slowly and dramatically or make a note in the margin. Also mark points at which you want to pause in the text or when you want to look at the audience.

Use clear, legible handwriting. Make sure that you write your letters large enough so that you can read them from the script easily when it is lying in front of you. If your script is already printed out you can enlarge the writing with the aid of a photocopier. Or choose a larger font on your computer.

The Cue Script

For most everyday speech situations a script offering cues is sufficient. You only make a note of the most important key concepts or the component parts of a sentence in the order in which you want to present them. To find the relevant cue in your script quickly it is important that you only note down a few cue words. Make sure the words are big and clear and you can recognise them quickly.

The first time they put together a script, many people make the mistake of noting down too many cue words. When they then look down at it during their speech or presentation they become irritated, not being able to find the correct continuation point because of the muddle of words. Having to scan a page in search of it makes them nervous and unnecessarily throws them off track.

Cue words are not abbreviated sentences, they are simply key concepts with which you can unlock the door to a new section or area of your speech. This is why it is not the quantity of cue words which is so important but their suitability.

When you have finished fleshing out your script, experiment by trying out your speech at home on your own. Record your speech and check your script by asking the following questions:

– Using your cue words, have you said everything you meant to say? If not, add the missing cue words.

– Was there a cue word that you found you did not need? If so, cross it off your script.

– Did nothing spring to mind when you read a cue word? This probably means that you have not chosen a suitable key concept. Find an appropriate key word or intimate a brief concept in two or three words.

You can also incorporate detailed sentences in your cue word script. This makes sense if you want to quote something word for word or if you want to give precise references.

Make sure that you check your speech for the following points:

Set the boundaries for the topic about which you are going to speak

When you plan your speech ask yourself the following questions to prevent yourself from getting bogged down.

– What is the occasion of your speech or presentation? Is its purpose to illuminate the audience, to express recognition and thanks, or to expound your own ideas?

– What is the most important thing to you about this subject?

– How can you best relate yourself, your opinion and your level of knowledge to the matter?

– To which interests and knowledge of the audience can you form a link?

Structuring the speech

At the beginning of your speech or your contribution to a discussion it is sensible to give your listeners some information that allows them to find their bearings.

This involves introducing yourself by name (perhaps also telling them what your function or your profession is). You do not need to introduce yourself if the person leading the discussion does this for you, someone else presents you or everybody knows who you are. If you do introduce yourself to an audience, note the following points:

– Do not commence your speech by giving your name, because your opening words can get lost in the initial general unrest. (Also see the section 'The Art of Speech', in particular the paragraph 'Warming Up'.)

– Pronounce your name loudly and slowly so that everybody can understand it.

– When mentioning your function, job or other personal details do not evaluate yourself using similar lines to the following: 'I'm only a housewife but I would still like to say something.'

A second way of helping your audience find their bearings is to categorise your speech. Let the audience know why you are talking, who has invited or asked you to speak, whether the subject of your speech is close to your heart or whether you would like to touch upon a particular aspect of a subject as an expert in that field. If the purpose of your speech is to show recognition or congratulate somebody then you can also briefly state in what relationship you stand to the person in question.

If you are giving a long lecture, especially if it is on a specialised subject or involves instructions, you can use a third method that will help your audience to find their bearings: let them know the structure of the speech that you have planned. You can give your audience an oral overview, something along the lines of 'Firstly I would like to explain XYZ. Secondly I would like to turn to this and that. And I shall then conclude by showing you how ABC can be achieved.' Or you can show the structure of your speech by using a flip chart or an overhead projector. (The use of flip charts and overhead projectors is explained in more detail in the section 'The Art of Speech'.)

The way you structure the core statements of what you have to say will mainly depend on the occasion and the object of your speech.

In the case of a technical or theoretical lecture or presentation it can be very useful to the listeners if you start by talking about something they are familiar with or if you link up what you have to say with their existing knowledge.

You could describe a problem that most people are familiar with from everyday situations, or could speak about experiences that many of the listeners may have in common with you. Starting with the concrete and familiar, you can then structure your text step by step so as to move on to something new or abstract.

Especially in the case of a technical or theoretical lecture or presentation, it can be enlivening if you do not just approach the subject from a factual–theoretical standpoint but also present yourself to the audience as a human being and make clear your own experiences and feelings on the subject-matter.

In the case of a speech that spells out a difference of opinions or positions taken in a debate, it may not just be a case of addressing technical questions but of setting out more general pro and contra positions. By way of introducing your speech or the contribution you wish to make to the discussion, you can describe the relevant problem from your point of view. Or you can start by summarising the opinions of your opponents in your own words before refuting them with your own arguments. You can start with the weakest argument and leave your strongest, most convincing argument till last, as the highlight, so to speak. At the end of your arguments, spell out the conclusion that you draw from them and the consequences that necessarily follow from them. In order to make your arguments seem more plausible for the listeners, you can enrich your speech by offering examples, facts, results of surveys and your own experiences. (More on this subject in the section 'All the Power in the World to Win People Over'.)

You can simplify your preparations for your speech or presentation if you keep on recording the parts that you are fleshing out as you go along. When you listen to the tape you will be able to hear what your concepts sound like. In the process a better way of expressing what you want to say might occur to you.

If you do not know exactly how to express a particular subject-matter in an appropriate way then make sure you formulate it in the most colloquial language. If in doubt, use everyday language and ignore formulations that are convoluted and complicated.

If you are well prepared for a speech it can make you self-assured. But on the other hand, make sure you do not spend too much time honing your speech. If you spend too much time preparing your speech it will set your nerves on edge. It is important that you are satisfied with your script, that you have fleshed it out and can bring your preparation to an end.

TAKING IN THE ROOM

Some speakers do not dare to look in to the audience when they start their speech. If they do look up after a couple of sentences they are thrown off track by the sudden sight of so many unfamiliar faces.

If you are going to hold your speech standing on a podium or from a lectern, then your view will be completely different from the view you would have if you were sitting in the audience. This is why we recommend that you get used to the sight of the room from where you are going to have to speak. Try to stand in this position or in the vicinity of it before it is your turn. Look at the audience from this position and get used to this viewpoint.

I personally like to arrive in the room where I am going to give a lecture early. I position myself at the front of the room, a little to the side, and watch the listeners as they enter one after another. I look at their faces and try to picture the audience. From the way that people enter the room and act I can see whether a lot of them know each other and are talking to each other or whether they have come alone, silently placing themselves on a chair. I can also gain some idea of what the acoustics in the room are like. From the chattering that gradually arises I can hear whether there is an echo in the room and whether rustling noises and the noise of chairs being shifted are muted by the carpet. In this way I sniff out the atmosphere slowly forming in the room. I find these precise observations very calming and I can put my 'feelers' out in order to feel in contact with the people and the surrounding room.

MAKING YOURSELF COMFORTABLE

Many women are at first baffled when we ask them whether they were sitting or standing comfortably during their first practice speech. For many, being comfortable has nothing to do with making a speech in front of an audience. On the contrary, most people assume feeling uncomfortable is part of giving a speech; that to feel a bit uncomfortable is even necessary. Holding this belief, many women either sit or stand in a tense posture long before it is their turn to speak. And most people manage to expend a lot of extra energy maintaining this muscle tension whilst waiting. However, this strain makes them more nervous, increasing their level of stress.

It is not necessary to have to cope with additional discomfort on top of having to deal with your task of giving a speech or presentation.

Despite the relatively prominent position you are in as a speaker, you can still make yourself comfortable. Here are a few tips on how to make yourself comfortable before and during your speech:

Make sure you avoid unpleasant people or situations prior to giving your speech

Avoid people and conditions that cause you unnecessary strain. Make sure you comfortably and safely reach where you are going to speak. If, as a driver, you are worried that traffic is going to put you on edge, take a taxi or use public transport. Avoid people who are nervous, anxious or angry. These emotions easily rub off.

Make sure you assume a relaxed posture

You can already make sure that you assume a straight but relaxed posture whilst standing or walking before you commence your speech.

Remind yourself to check your posture from time to time: make sure that you do not strain any body muscles unnecessarily. Try to relax your face as well. Some people do not realise how tensed up their jaw, forehead or neck muscles are. This can cause headaches.

Dress appropriately and comfortably

Wear clothes that do not make you feel restricted. Dress in such a way that you do not need to pay attention to whether your skirt, blouse or belt sits properly. Things that easily slip or feel alienating cause unnecessary discomfort. It is sensible to make sure that your clothing is not only suitable for the occasion but that it fits well and that you feel comfortable in it.

In our seminars we have frequently observed how women wearing high heels have an unsteady gait. When a speaker approaches a lectern in her high heels, even if she is only tottering slightly in them, it is noticeable. If she is also wearing a tight skirt she will also take short, rapid steps. Wearing high heels frequently affects posture, causing strain on your legs (in particular your fibula muscles) and your pelvic area. For this reason we recommend to the participants in our sessions that they wear flat shoes in which they can walk with self-assurance and assume a relaxed posture in front of their audience.

Shut out anything that disturbs you

When you begin speaking in front of an audience, again, make sure you make everything as comfortable for yourself as possible. Arrange everything on the lectern as best you can. If necessary, make sure that the microphone is in the correct position so that you don't need to bend down or strain your neck in order to speak into it. If there is anything else that bothers you, ask for assistance before you begin. If the noise from the street is too loud, have the windows closed and you can also close the door leading to the corridor.

Your audience may have to wait for a moment whilst you arrange everything around you. There is nothing wrong with this, since it shows that you take your role as a speaker seriously.

WELCOMING YOUR BODY'S SIGNALS

If you are not accustomed to holding speeches, if it is not part of your everyday routine and you only ever do it now and again, then you will experience this situation as something special. That is to say, you will probably become aware of feelings and bodily sensations that signal you are doing something out of the ordinary. Holding a speech is a different experience from going shopping or brushing your teeth, that's why it is reasonable that you are curious as to what it will be like or feel agitated. Please do not try to eliminate or dismiss these feelings. Do not fight against what your body wants to offer you in the way of help. Experiencing an edgy feeling or your heart's pounding are signals that your body is 'playing along'. Your brain, your heart and your circulation, your muscles and nerves are attuning themselves to your special purpose. Be conscious of what is going on inside you and welcome these physical changes.

Holding a speech and staying completely cool and absolutely unaffected is just not going to happen. Fortunately, in the true sense of the words, you will present in body as well as soul.

THE ART OF SPEECH

THE MESSAGES OF BODY LANGUAGE

We express various aspects of our being with our bodies. You see the following in the way people gesticulate, in their facial expressions, in their posture and the way they move:

- their mental state

- gender-specific differences

- social status or to which section of society someone belongs

- cultural differences

In our book we are primarily concerned with the aspects of body language that concern women – in particular women who want to speak in front of other people.

To begin with we would like to offer an example of how typically female body language is acquired in the course of childhood.

Little girls of three or five years old do not find it easy to assert themselves in front of adults or other siblings. Many experience that they are more likely to get what they want if they behave in a manner in which adults would like to see them behave: as a little, cute, good girl. Girls often learn that it is to their advantage if they want to achieve something to tilt their heads slightly when they speak, give a little smile and raise their voices.

Back in our childhood, this body language of the 'cute little girl' had its effect. We were able to get our way now and again by doing this. In any case most of the time we were better off doing this than stamping our foot and causing a tantrum, shouting 'But I want'. The cute girl way got results, and having been stamped in your memory it becomes a habit. This is why even though we may be 35 or 45 we tilt our head, suddenly raise the pitch of our voice and smile if we want to succeed in getting something across. Most of the time we do not notice (in particular we are not conscious that we raise the pitch of our voice) if our body language automatically changes – out of habit. Because of these experiences, the people who are involved in a discussion or the listeners also see a little girl standing in front of them, smiling and saying 'Please, please', and not the adult woman who is serious about herself and what she is saying.

There is in fact a difference between whether a woman is conscious of her body language and whether she uses a certain amount of charm or friendliness on purpose to pursue her interests, or whether she wears a 'be fond of me' smile on every occasion, whether it is appropriate or not. If the female 'be fond of me' expression is a habit that is unconscious it can easily happen that this habit becomes a kind of 'self-sabotage'. Time and again it happens to women that they undermine the seriousness and the significance of their speech by making themselves small and using cute body language.

This is an example from a seminar as to how to find your own body language:

A participant was practising a speech in which she wanted to convince the members of a committee that speed restrictions should be introduced in particular residential areas. When she reached the most important part of her speech, her words were forceful but at the same time she looked down and in short, sharp movements repeatedly raised her shoulders. In our culture, the action of raising the shoulders signifies, 'I don't know' or 'I'm not sure'. By coupling her 'I don't know' gesture with her lowered gaze she sabotaged the expressiveness of her words. In speaking she expressed resolute demands whilst her body expressed a certain element of doubt. She herself was not aware of this. Shrugging her shoulders was just a habit, something that she almost imperceptibly always did when she was speaking. It was not until she saw herself on video in the seminar that she realised how much this little gesture undermined her power to convince.

It is difficult to stop doing particular ingrained gestures. Most of the time it looks very stiff if people attempt to gain control over parts of their body. For most people it is easier to substitute the habitual gesture for a new and more appropriate one. The woman described above tried out different gestures and movements when she talked and then watched the result on video. She discovered that if she stood up straight and pulled her shoulders back, this made a much more forceful and convincing impression and also suited her. At the appropriate points in her speech she looked at her listeners and pushed her shoulders back, raising her upper body slightly. Now her body language was in tune with what she was saying.

By briefly checking her movements and making sure that she was conscious of her posture before and during the most decisive parts of her speech, the participant was able to remind herself of her new body language when it was necessary to do so.

On observing body language it is noticeable that women (as opposed to men) assume a posture that tends to be very economical in terms of taking up space. When they are sitting they usually cross their legs, so that only one foot usually touches the floor. Their arms are close to their bodies, their heads are ducked and their shoulders appear to be smaller because they are bent forwards or are slightly raised. Stretched out arms that extend to the armrests of a chair, a chin that looks out into the world and a comfortable leg position typify the male posture.

Body language is not only something that is rehearsed and learnt, but also expresses our mental state. Twiddling your hair and chewing your bottom lip are gestures expressing embarrassment and insecurity. In the case of many women, these different aspects of body language converge: what has been learnt, what has become a habit and the mental expression. They have learnt gestures and modes of conduct with which they express insecurity and self-belittlement. The habitual gestures and modes of conduct do not just have an effect on people with whom they are holding a discussion or on their listeners; their posture affects themselves as well. A self-belittling body language may be the original cause for feeling insecure and experiencing self-doubt, or it may exacerbate it.

If you are feeling anxious and small, standing up straight and showing presence will give you inner strength. The self-assurance that is conveyed by your body also comes back at you. Try the following exercise:

Exercise: The Way to Achieve more Forceful Posture

Seat yourself in a chair or armchair that gives you courage. If you are more inclined to associate the word courage with a warlike doggedness and tenseness, then perhaps think of 'confidence' or 'inner strength' instead.

Seat yourself in such a way that you convey confidence and inner strength. Remain in this posture and make sure that you rid yourself of any muscle tension, but do not let yourself go limp. In other words sit up straight but do not tense up. You can try being active in this position, talking or conversing; you do not need to sit absolutely still. Once you have got in touch with your courage, confidence and inner strength, this will be conveyed to your movements. Try the same thing when standing or walking. You will find that posture and movements that express a feeling of confidence on the outside at the same time strengthen you on the inside.

To conclude take a sort of inner photograph of your courageous, strong conduct. Try to store the sensation of how your body feels in your memory. You will then be able to assume this state of conduct before and during a speech.

GAINING ATTENTION

You have probably also experienced the following. You are listening to a lecture or a speech and you are pretty sure that it is about something extremely interesting. But unfortunately the whole thing is presented in such a boring and uninteresting way that you can barely listen. The monotonous flow of words sends you off to sleep, your thoughts wander and there is nothing else in the room that is capable of grabbing your attention. You ask yourself how long this lecture is going to go on.

If a speech or lecture is presented in a boring way, the speaker is often the last person to realise. The speaker is much too engrossed in giving his or her speech to notice the little tell-tale signs that people are not paying attention. Some are yawning, some are reading their notes, people are whispering in the back row, or they are slumped in their chairs and are staring at the ceiling or the floor. As a rule, if listeners are bored, they will be quiet about it, making their boredom barely noticeable. We would like to offer you a few tips about how to make your speech more interesting and lively.

Intelligibility

An audience quickly loses interest if large chunks of what you are saying are unintelligible. This may not be due just to the fact that you are speaking quietly or not clearly, but may also be because the contents of your speech are too complicated or abstract. In particular, if you are talking on a subject as a specialist or expert and you know your subject-matter well, you easily run the danger of using technical terms that some listeners will not understand. You will probably just talk about things in a matter-of-fact way, not realising that not everybody may understand you. Even when you are speaking in front of specialists and fellow colleagues it can be useful to explain the odd foreign word or abstract process. Amongst themselves, specialists do not have universal knowledge either.

You can improve the intelligibility of what you are saying if you apply a few general tricks that I am now going to introduce you to. Check whether any of these ideas are suitable for your speech.

Give examples

If you give examples from everyday life you will be able to create a link with what the listeners already know. This is also a good way of explaining abstract processes or theories.

Use pictorial language, analogies, metaphors

Some processes are more easily described by using pictures. If for example, I talk about the 'carousel of fear rotating more quickly', then this is a pictorial expression for the increase of fear. A metaphor, for example, is the concept 'inner rule'. These words use an intelligible term to describe the mental process with which people put themselves under pressure.

Use visual aids

Flip charts and overhead projectors (that are also called daylight projectors) are especially useful for presentations. A flip chart is a kind of stand-up board with a large paper pad. You can draw graphics with a thick felt-tip pen, noting down cue words or individual points that you want to speak about for everyone to see. It is important that you write or draw clearly, so that people who are sitting at a distance will also be able to see it. The use of a flip chart is only recommended if your audience consists of 25 people or fewer. If more people are listening to you it is more sensible to use an overhead projector. Of course, you can use this with a smaller group, for a discussion amongst colleagues, for example, but it is particularly useful in large auditoriums or rooms. For the machine you need transparent folios that you can obtain from a stationery shop, where you can also purchase the special (colour) pens with which you can write on the folios. You can, however, also copy typed tests or other drawings onto folios with a photocopier.

Whether you use a flip chart or an overhead projector, you should keep in mind that you should not write too much on a page since people may not be able to read the information if it is written too small. Also, putting too much information on it may confuse your listeners rather than be helpful. Some speakers make the mistake of turning away from the audience and towards the flip chart page or folio when they are explaining something. Generally this means that your listeners will hardly be able to hear you. If you are going to explain a flip chart or folio to an audience make sure that you are standing next to the machine, and speak towards the audience.

If you are going to use these kinds of aids it is important that you leave enough time before your speech to check whether everything is in working order and you know how to use it all.

Announcing the structure of your speech

In particular if you are going to give a long speech, it is easier for the listeners to follow if you announce what the structure of your speech is going to be – for example, by naming the points you wish to discuss at the beginning of your speech. It is even better if you put your structure on an overhead projector or a flip chart for everybody to see. Whilst you are giving your speech you can then mark each point you refer to in turn. If you get stuck in the course of your speech you can find your bearings again simply by taking a quick glance at the folio or flip chart.

Clear pronunciation

Sometimes speakers cannot be understood because their pronunciation is not clear. Particularly if the acoustics are not very good in the room, for example, if there is interference (such as traffic noise) or because there is no carpet and the scraping of chairs echoes loudly, it is important that you speak slowly and clearly. In order that your voice carries across the whole room it is useful to imagine that you are trying to reach the opposite wall with your words. Place emphasis on speaking more slowly, much more slowly than you are accustomed to, pausing briefly between sentences.

On the whole your pronunciation becomes clearer if you place emphasis on speaking more slowly and you do not let your words run into each other, but pronounce them individually.

In rare cases the cause of unclear pronunciation is a speech impediment. If this is the case it is advisable to consult a specialist, someone skilled in speech therapy or speech training.

Making your presence felt

In the first instance, the art of gaining attention lies in simply being attentive yourself. An audience will pay attention to you if you yourself look at its members attentively. You can already gain attention prior to commencing your speech when you step in front of the lectern or step on to the podium simply by radiating calmness and making your presence felt.

Many speakers throw away the few moments they are given before commencing their speech by hurrying up to the lectern, shuffling the pages of their manuscript and saying their first words without even looking at the audience, as if its members are not important. It is very probable that this kind of preamble gets lost in the general unrest because the audience is just as uncomposed as the speaker and is unprepared for the forthcoming speech.

You can make an entrance at the beginning of your speech by doing the following:

– Walking and moving in a calm and composed manner.

– Making sure you assume a straight and relaxed posture before you start to speak.

– Looking at your listeners (smile if you like).

If people are restless in the room you can maintain your attentiveness and look at the audience until the people present realise that you are about to begin and settle down.

Warming up

In addition to beginning your speech calmly and with presence, you must also remember that your voice and intonation are important generators of attention. Listeners require a minute or two to attune to your voice. You yourself as a speaker need a little time to get used to the way your voice sounds in the room and to figure out how loudly you need to speak. You and your audience tune into each other in much the same way as you tune into a radio station. Everybody involved requires your first few minutes of speech in order to get attuned. Allow yourself a few minutes to warm up and your listeners a few minutes to get used to your voice. It is better not to make core statements or other important remarks during this period of attunement. Open your speech with a welcome, with a few nice words, or by expressing thanks for being invited. If you want to give a committed, provocative speech you can start by explaining how you came to hold your view or what provoked you to talk on the subject. After you have warmed up you will probably have managed to get rid of any 'frogs' or 'lumps' in your throat and will now be able to turn to your principal statements more competently.

DEVELOPING YOUR OWN STYLE OF SPEECH

Two aspects of communication are expressed in your style of speech: your own personality – who you are – and the external effect of speaking – the sort of effect you have on others.

In many traditional speaking courses the focus is simply on the external factor of making a speech sound effective. The aspects of speaking relating to its being a form of self-representation and an expression of the way you are, are, for the most part, ignored. Fostering an individual style of speech may also contribute to the development of your personality.

In most cases women (and also men) who suffer from a fear of speaking do not like the way they talk. At first many of the women who participate in our seminars think that their voices, movements and facial expressions when they speak are 'simply horrifying'. Especially when they see a video recording of themselves for the first time, they get the impression that their style of speech is 'frightful'.

In general there is a distinct connection between the extent of stage fright and a rejection of one's own way of speaking. The more a woman believes that her way of speaking is wrong or inadequate, the more frightened she will be of speaking in front of a group. And this fear has the effect of making her speak quickly, unclearly or monotonously, which she in turn finds 'ghastly'.

This circle of self-rejection and fear produces an effect like a large lid; it covers and suppresses your personal style of speech. If on the other hand your stage fright abates, the lid can be lifted and an effective, highly individual manner of speaking comes to the fore. Women who previously, on account of their stage fright, spoke without moving often start gesticulating and changing their facial expressions. Others, on the other hand, who had a tendency to make nervous and sudden movements in their state of fear become calmer in their movements when they are not scared.

Most people are much less tense when their fear abates; they see and hear more of the audience, pay more attention to their own thoughts and feelings when they are speaking and can react more appropriately when something unforeseen happens during their speech or presentation. But, above all, individuals find that they are more sympathetic towards the way they speak. With this their courage to experiment with their style of speech grows.

You will also have an individual style of speech that will come to the fore if you speak in front of or with people without experiencing fear. Try paying attention to how you speak when you recount an experience to your relatives, colleagues or friends, that is, in a situation where there is no fear. In these kinds of unforced speech situations most people have a very individual way of speaking.

Once your stage fright diminishes you will find it much easier to speak in front of a group of people using your own individual style of speech. And you can use this style in a flexible manner according to what you are aiming for in your speech and depending on the particular situation. If, for example, you are introducing a new concept during a discussion with colleagues in your company, you will behave and speak in a different way from the way you would if you were explaining a game to the little guests at a child's birthday party. Your style of speech is not so much a pattern of behaviour that is fixed, but more a reservoir of possible ways of expressing yourself.

If you have had little opportunity of familiarising yourself with your own style of speech and developing it, make sure you create opportunities for yourself in which you can experiment. To begin with, you can think about whether there are more opportunities you can seize in your everyday existence that allow you to make a contribution or hold a little speech. Maybe opportunities of this kind will present themselves at your workplace, in a further training course, in an organised discussion or a celebration amongst family or friends. Even if you are still not sure whether you are a really good speaker, try to give yourself the chance to speak on a day-to-day basis.

You can also carry out a few experiments with regard to the way you speak, either at home on your own or in a small group. With the help of a video camera you can accurately study your manner of speech. A lot of households already own video cameras, but you could also hire one. Make sure that you do not tear each other apart whilst experimenting with it. Try out different ways of speaking.

Exercise: Speaking Differently

One at a time, try some new ways of speaking:

- Alter the pace at which you speak, first more quickly and then much more slowly than you are accustomed to. Then incorporate speaking slowly and quickly in the same act of speaking. Pay attention to which speed suits you better and the difference in effect between talking more slowly and talking more quickly.

- Perhaps you are accustomed to making certain movements when you speak. Often these are movements that you only notice when you see yourself on video. See what happens if you stop gesticulating altogether.

- Focus on your facial expressions. Talk as if you were relating the story of an exciting fairy tale and let the drama play on your features so that it is reflected in your face.

- Read out a text repeatedly, trying out different pitches of voice. Let your voice become a little deeper without making too much of an effort. Try speaking in a higher, louder or quieter voice.

Do not view this exercise as being an 'obligatory' rhetorical exercise, but as a motivating and loosening-up exercise to broaden your speaking experiences. In the process you may discover a way of speaking that you like and which sounds good to other people. Keep experimenting with new variations. After a while you will discover that you prefer particular ways of speaking and that they suit you better than others. And above all, with the aid of video recordings, you will be able to get to know which way of speaking is more likely to attract the attention of an audience and how to express yourself clearly.

POSITIVE SELF-IMAGE

If you are talking on a particular subject as an expert then let the audience know that you are an expert. Most people are more likely to believe a person of authority or an expert than somebody who is not an expert. People believe in what experts such as scientists, engineers, politicians and so on, say even when they talk about things on which they are not expert. Unfortunately in public men still have an advantage over women, that is, if a man and woman who are equally competent experts speak, the man will generally be considered the more competent expert – even by women.

The advantage that men have over women is augmented by the fact that many women have more of a tendency than men to understate their case and not reveal their abilities. Many women begin what they have to say by making a type of self-deprecatory remark, for example by

– making an apology for speaking up: 'I'm sorry, but I'd like to say something on the subject as well.'

– belittling their knowledge: 'I don't know that much about this subject, but I'd still like to say ...'

– devaluing their speech contribution: 'Well I suppose everything has already been said, but I would just like to ...'

Women often find it more difficult than men to present themselves in a positive light. The fear of being considered a show-off or impostor already sets in when they have to refer to their own specialised knowledge or experiences. Many women would prefer it if people were just able to identify their achievements and capabilities without having to be told.

On the other hand, most women find it extremely easy to portray themselves in a negative light. Their weaknesses, faults and mishaps are an endless source of conversation.

When we ask women to report on their faults, weaknesses and mishaps in our seminars, most women are able to talk about them for at least and hour or more. If on the other hand they are asked to talk about their abilities, their successes and talents, then a lot of women run out of things to say after a couple of minutes.

An inner rule along the lines of 'self-praise stinks' is going to prevent you from saying anything good about yourself, prevent you from revealing your abilities and talking about your achievements and successes. This inner muzzle leads many women to believe that they are only really being honest and open towards others if they reveal themselves together with their weaknesses and faults. If on the other hand they reveal their achievements and successes, many feel as if they are being dishonest or lying.

There is a purpose to this form of self-deprecation in communication. If women remain in the background and only reveal their weaknesses, it ensures that their conversation partners will feel as little rivalry or jealousy as possible towards them. In addition, this allows their conversation partners in the room to step into the foreground and to talk positively about themselves. Because women accept or even admire their opposites, they create an (apparently) harmonious and uncompetitive relationship with their conversation partners. From this point of view women's absent positive self-image is also a communication strategy (more likely to be unconscious) that ensures harmony in relationships. The price that women pay is their devaluation – in the eyes of themselves and of others.

This inability to present themselves in a positive light is particularly disadvantageous for women in professional or business situations, since self-advertising is part of the job.

Women in these positions who avoid presenting their abilities and experiences in a positive light quickly fall behind their colleagues and rivals. For this reason what happens is that women efficiently and competently master the tasks they have to deal with, but other people get the credit – often the people who are better at presenting themselves – in the form of salary rises and public recognition.

If you want to avoid hiding your light under a bushel when making a speech, practise presenting yourself in a positive light beforehand. To begin with, take all the achievements and abilities that you yourself consider to be normal and think are not worth mentioning, and see them as something special. It is not until you yourself consider that your achievements and abilities are something positive that you can present yourself in a positive way to others.

Here are some suggestions about how you can present yourself in a positive light.

Exercise: Presenting Yourself in a Positive Light

– Make a positive list: Note down your abilities, talents, successes and achievements. Include everything that you are proud of, that you have done well and can do well. We are not just concerned with outstanding successes, but above all the abilities that allow you to cope in everyday situations. If you want to present yourself in a positive light on a particular occasion (for example in a specialised lecture or an interview) then you can specifically prepare yourself in the area you require with this kind of list.

– Keep a positive diary: Particularly when you think you have achieved hardly anything positive and think that you have been unsuccessful in your everyday existence, it can be useful to consider your daily activities over a longer period of time in a new light. At the end of a day write down exactly what you have managed to do and what you have done well. Make a point of watching out for the small things and things you take for granted; do not forget to note them down. Only make a note of positive achievements and abilities; ignore criticism, things that highlight what you perceive as your limitations, or that make you feel devalued.

– Talk positively about yourself: Start talking to other people about your abilities and successes. If you tend to present yourself with your weaknesses and faults, it is particularly important that you find the words to express your positive sides. To begin with, it can be useful to practise positive self-presentation in conversations. Take the opportunity to say something good about yourself now and again.

THE COURAGE TO VOICE YOUR OWN OPINIONS

Many women shy away from expressing their beliefs when speaking. Some women feel that such behaviour is too brusque and harsh.

A participant in one of our seminars had developed a very plausible argument for a better way of promoting women in companies and departments during a practice speech. But at the end of her speech, instead of making a demand and reinforcing her opinion, she simply tagged the sentence on to the end of her speech: 'Wouldn't it be nice if women had the same influence as men?' This was a feeble end to a speech in comparison with the rousing argument that the participant had so ingeniously developed.

When the woman saw herself on video she thought that her last sentence seemed strangely weak compared to the rest of her speech. Her speech had been very fierce and critical, but she wanted to appear a little more friendly at the end of her speech; she did not want to leave the audience with the impression that she was a hard-bitten campaigner.

Many women find it difficult to display their expressive strength and ability in front of an audience. If they present what they are talking about in a committed and decisive manner they often find themselves on a collision course with their inner rules. For example, 'You must be affable and diplomatic and not act like a charging bull.' This led in the instance just described to the words 'Wouldn't it be nice if?' which undermined the conclusion of what was otherwise a fiery speech.

Researchers in linguistics such as Senta Trömel-Plötz and others have pointed out that women (as opposed to men) tend to speak more carefully.

This involves

- using economical expressions such as 'maybe', 'possibly', 'roughly', 'a little', 'presumably', 'somehow'

- transforming a statement into a question by adding the words 'isn't it?' or 'don't you think?'

- formulating sentences in such a way that they are first-person sentences, for example, 'In my opinion ...' or 'I think ...' or 'I believe ...'

Men on the other hand often tend to take the more direct approach of 'This is the way the world is' although they are not as sure on the inside as they appear to be on the outside.

Men are usually much less careful and critical about expressing their opinions in speeches, conversations and discussions than women are. In public, the male benchmarks of speaking successfully are self-assurance, clarity and the ability to lead – benchmarks recognised by both men and women. According to this norm, women who are vague and who resort to using economical expressions give the impression of being insecure and ignorant.

However, if women depart from this 'female' way of speaking and start to talk in a more masculine manner – 'There is nothing to be said against what I am saying' – then they easily fall prey to being judged as harsh and aggressive. So the apparent opinionlessness of women is also an indication of the dilemma they are faced with. Public speaking easily becomes a type of balancing act between, on the one hand, being charming, feminine, but because of this appearing less effective and, on the other, the 'This is the way the world is' way of speaking which in the case of women is often interpreted as unfeminine, harsh and dogged. And many women want to reveal their opinions in their speech but do not want to force them down people's throats or anger them. This results in a combination of wanting to express their opinion on the one side and wanting to appear harmless and cute on the other in order to maintain a positive relationship with the audience.

It is possible that they have an automatic and unconscious tendency (like many other women) to tone down when they are speaking.

In order to prevent this they do not necessarily have to resort to a masculine way of speaking. It is often very helpful to think about your beliefs before you get up to speak. Otherwise you are faced with the danger of being, as it were, caught out whilst you are giving your speech or presentation and thereby revealing that you do not stand by your supposed convictions. In other words, subliminally you will signal to the audience that you are not really saying what you believe in. The impression your audience then gains is that, although you are making an effort, you do not sound very credible.

On the other hand, if you stand by what you are saying you can develop a special kind of radiance that is difficult to acquire through training. Your body language, voice and the way you present yourself will all be in tune and form an appropriate unity. Also, speaking convincingly about what you yourself recognise as being good and right takes up a lot less energy. To sell to an audience an opinion of which you yourself are not convinced requires an enormous amount of energy and a lot of acting ability.

Make sure that you do not belittle yourself or soften your statements at the end of your speech by, for example, offering an apology or questioning everything that you have just said. Sometimes it is useful to summarise your core statements in short, brief sentences at the end of your speech, or to conclude by expressing a wish for the future or a request.

Irrespective of which conclusion you choose, please do not just let your speech peter out by standing up and collecting up your papers whilst saying your final words and then making a quick departure, saying something like 'Well, that was it.' Try to make a calm and collected exit. When you say your last words, make sure you assume an upright position but that your posture is nevertheless relaxed. Look at the audience when you have finished your speech and remain sitting or standing for a little while. Only then calmly return to your seat.

ALL THE POWER IN THE WORLD TO WIN PEOPLE OVER

Arguing has very little to do with fighting, and has more to do with winning people over and enticing other people to our intentions and opinions. Good arguments are like magnets that are capable of changing the direction of thoughts. The only way this is possible is if our opponents are willing to change their minds, which is something that can only occur on a voluntary basis. Let me say right away: if your opponents are unwilling to change their opinions, then irrespective of how good your arguments are you will not be able to win them over to your cause. But we rarely encounter the attitude of 'I do not want to change' in everyday life. Often people only appear to be unchangeable. With a little skill and the right key arguments it is possible to break open even the trickiest of safes. What you require most of all is perseverance. Do not give up until you have tested your skills as thoroughly as you can. But what actually constitutes a good argument? And how should you talk so that your listeners enjoy listening to you? If your cause and your aim are of particular importance to you then take the time to prepare your relevant arguments. Now for a number of practical tips that will help you to do this.

Your Goal

You will only be able to change people's opinions if your aim is clear. The first person you convince is yourself. If you are in conflict with yourself you may radiate this doubt and affect other people with it. If you are not convinced yourself, others will feel encouraged to argue against you. The more transparent your goal and the more you yourself are convinced, the more forceful and convincing your argument will appear from the outside. Before you commence speaking, set your boundaries. Think about where you are prepared to give way and where you want to stand your ground.

The practical preparation

- Take your time and think about what the best result would be.

- Of what do you want to convince the others?

- What do you want to achieve with your listeners?

- What do you want absolutely and where can you afford to give way?

Developing Suitable Arguments

Emphasis should be placed on the word suitable. A convincing argument should be suitable for your listeners or your opponent. It should be suited to the thoughts and views of the people you wish to convince. This is exactly the point at which some people make a mistake. They use arguments that convince themselves. But often these arguments are not capable of convincing the listeners. An example: imagine that a salesman wants to sell you a video recorder. Two arguments seem convincing to you. Firstly: he is working on a commission basis so he will get a percentage if he sells you the video recorder. Secondly: he requires storage space for new machines. Taking this into account it would be a good thing if he could sell you the machine. Two brilliant arguments – but only for the salesman. He is hardly going to be able to convince you to buy it for this reason. The salesman would only be able to convince you with arguments that coincide with your interests and views. His task would now be to discover how he could win you over. And what is going to convince you is different from what motivates him. Perhaps you will let yourself be convinced by the argument that the machine is easy to use and programme. Convincing arguments offer the listener a benefit or an advantage. So it is important that you know what may be useful to the person standing opposite you. The better you know the people you want to convince the easier it will be to develop appropriate arguments.

The practical preparation

– The more benefits and advantages for the listeners you address, the more power you will have to convince.

– Develop beneficial arguments. To what extent is what you want beneficial to the listeners?

Making Sure that the Atmosphere is Positive

Avoid arguments and confrontations. To convince other people means getting a learning process going in the listeners. People only change their minds voluntarily and in a positive atmosphere. If the conversational atmosphere becomes rawer, people's attitudes will be hardened and they will stick to their opinions, they may even become more adamant about them. For this reason avoid getting into a battle of words. React towards your listeners' counter-arguments with understanding. Make an effort to assume a 'yes' attitude even when the person opposite you has got a completely different opinion.

The practical preparation

– What kind of counter-arguments are the listeners going to come up with?

– Arm yourself in advance and think about possible ways of responding to these counter-arguments.

– How can you express appreciation, yet at the same time present your own opinion?

Assembling Your Arguments

The more arguments you can find in support of your position the longer you will be able to speak about it and convince people of it. If you only have one or two arguments then you will quickly run out of ammunition. Having more arguments means that you will have the advantage of a much longer broadcasting time. Sometimes listeners expect you to invest a lot of time in trying to convince them. The more time that is taken for opinions to go back and forth the greater the likelihood that there will be a positive outcome. But do not be worried if you cannot think of many arguments. You can repeat each argument several times. Sometimes a convincing argument only sinks in if it is repeated several times over, like an advertisement that is shown repeatedly. List your arguments in the order of importance and how persuasive they are. Make sure you assume the viewpoint of the people or person you are trying to convince. Your most important and convincing arguments will be beneficial or advantageous to the listeners. But you will need all the cards in a pack, as you do in a game of scat. The ones of lower value also belong to the game.

The practical preparation

– Assemble all the arguments that you can think of. The big and the little arguments.

– What arguments do you have for your purposes?

Developing Your Argument Strategy

If you are pursuing a larger goal, then prepare yourself for the fact that you will have to speak about it on more than one occasion. Frequently several discussions or negotiations take place before something important is decided upon. There is also a warming-up period for arguing. Do not start with your best argument. Save your most powerful arguments for now. Perhaps your listeners will meet your aims with scepticism. There is nothing wrong with this. To begin with build up a positive relationship towards the person or people you are speaking to. If you show people genuine goodwill and are friendly towards them they are more likely to change. If you wish to bring about a change it is especially important that you do not condemn outright what you are seeking to change along the lines of 'What you have done up until now is a load of rubbish, but now I am going to make my brilliant suggestion.' Often this is what is said even if with more refined or delicate words. If you do this you are attacking the listeners. If you want to win people over then do not alienate them. Look over previous goings-on and pick out something that you show genuine recognition for or can accept. Tell the listeners what you find good, what you like and then make them aware of your own personal interest in the matter. Call your aim a 'suggestion' or a 'request'. This sounds less oppressive than a 'demand'.

The practical preparation

– For longer speeches or frequent discussions arrange your arguments in the order of their importance and power.

– What are your most powerful arguments, what are the weakest? Start with a weaker argument.

– If you wish to implement changes, express honest recognition for the good aspects of what you seek to change. Only then offer your suggestions for change.

HOW TO ARGUE CONVINCINGLY AND TO THE POINT

We would now like to introduce you to a very simple and effective method of setting out your aims and speaking convincingly. In our training sessions we have seen that women who have thoroughly prepared their speech or presentation often insist on throwing away the arguments they have put together so carefully. They do this all at once. All their preparation is reeled off in a flash, all their arguments are rattled off in quick succession. The listeners are snowed under. Nobody gains anything from this. The listeners are overfed and the speaker has reeled off her most convincing arguments without producing any great effect. For the listeners it is important that they can reconstruct their thought processes. You will only be able to alter the way people think if what you say sounds convincing. In the case of small conversations or discussions it will suffice simply to say what you want and back this up with a reason, for example, 'I suggest that we make a new arrangement so we don't have to keep on talking about it. I would like to make the following suggestion ...' If something very important is at stake, then a cleverer plan of action may be called for. You raise your concern one step at a time and slowly entice your listeners over to your way of thinking. This step-by-step procedure will be particularly helpful for you if you have a tendency to lose your thread in the excitement. You can build up a speech or contribution to a discussion logically in four steps and in the correct order. Start by describing the problem or the point from which you wish to proceed and reveal your suggestion only at the end. This has the advantage that everybody will listen to you until the end in order to discover what you are getting at. We shall now discuss the four-step strategy with a few proposals on how you can formulate the individual steps.

The Four-Step Strategy

1. *The starting point* (the occasion of your speaking):

   What is the occasion? Why do you want the conversation?
   (For example: 'I'm here because ...', 'It is about ...', 'I would like to speak to you about ...')

2. *Briefly addressing the problem or the question*:

   What is it that is wrong? Or what does the problem look like?
   ('Recently the following questions have arisen ...', 'At present we lack ...', 'I am sure that you have already noticed that ...')

3. *Facts and experiences*:

   Which facts and experiences are important here?
   ('The fact is ...', 'It looks as if ...', 'As far as I know ...')

4. *Consequence, conclusion, suggest a solution*:

   What follows from it? What are the consequences? What kind of solutions and suggestions do you have to offer?
   ('We can draw the conclusion that ...', 'From this we can conclude that it is necessary ...', 'I think we could resolve the problem by ...')

With the help of these four steps you can hold a long speech. At each step say a few sentences. Or by just saying a short sentence at each of these steps you can still make a valid contribution to a discussion. In the first three steps you have the opportunity to establish the approval of the listeners. Describe the question or the problem in such a way that as many people as possible are able to agree with you. People who have already said yes to something are more open to anything further you say. You already have your foot in the door. If your facts and experiences meet with approval in the third step then the chances of your consequences and conclusions in the fourth step being accepted are greater. Your argument has hit the mark.

As with all the other rhetorical methods and techniques that we offer you in this book, you can adapt the four-step strategy to suit yourself and your own style of speech.

HOW TO DEAL EFFECTIVELY WITH OBJECTIONS AND COUNTER-ARGUMENTS

You can be pleased about any counter-arguments offered. This shows that your words have been registered and that people have thought about them. It would be really sad if nobody opposed anything you said and yet at the same time failed to take up any of your suggestions. With counter-arguments you can find out what the listeners still need. What is the opposition not yet convinced about? What have you not explained properly? Which considerations have you not thought of yet? Counter-arguments can reveal this information. Opposition on the part of your listeners serves as a pointer to an even more effective argument. You need certain tools to be able to deal with counter-arguments, abilities that enable you to react in a flexible and creative manner.

Listen

Listening attentively is just as important as finding suitable arguments when you are trying to convince someone. Absorb what your opponent counters your argument with; do not attempt to refute it straight away. It is important that you listen without working yourself up into an agitated state. Try to understand the other person. Creep up to the counter-argument. What does your opponent want? Have they any secret fears? Are they experiencing any problems because of what you want? Try to sound out what lies behind the objection. And do not already try to put together your own counter-arguments whilst silently considering the objection. Instead lie in ambush.

Ask the Right Questions

Have you really understood the opposing opinion? Do you know exactly why your opponent holds a certain opinion? We have a tendency to make up for missing information by inferring things.

Instead of being inquisitive, we start by attributing opinions to the other person. It is better to ask before you catch yourself doing this. Find out what the opposing opinion is. Examine the background: 'In your opinion, is there a better way?', 'What would you do if you were in my position?', 'How to do you imagine the whole thing?' Keep asking questions until you feel you understand your opponent. This does not apply to interruptions and heckles whilst you are actually giving your speech. Anybody who shouts their opposing opinion at you whilst you are speaking is causing a disruption and does not deserve any further attention. Leave the questioning for a later time, perhaps where you can talk amongst yourselves. Only if you want to get to the bottom of these heckles, that is.

In a discussion, asking questions is often a good way of taking on leadership. The person who asks, leads. This way you can prevent an exchange of blows in which everybody talks past one another and nobody really understands one another. Your good arguments would fizzle out and be ineffective. Make sure that your questions really are answered. Keep on asking questions until you have entirely understood the person who holds the opposing opinion. If new information emerges of which you were previously unaware, make sure that it does not unnerve you. If your previous argument is no longer suitable, ask for time to reflect. This may be a break of several minutes or a week in which to reflect on your concern. Suggest a time for further discussion.

The 'Yes and' Answer

If you have understood the opposing opinion, try to accept it in as positive a way as you can. Do not let yourself immediately be dragged into a discussion of the counter-arguments. If you do this you could get yourself tangled up in them without having really examined the opposing opinion properly. Besides, a quick response to a counter-reaction may trigger off an equally quick counter-response. Before you know it you will be in the thick of an exchange of blows, similar to a game of ping pong. Usually the only thing achieved by such an exchange is a flaring of emotions, with remarks and comments becoming ever more agitated. Eventually the point is reached at which all anybody cares about is winning, with nobody bothering to listen properly any more. To convince people, you need goodwill, understanding and the ability to comprehend thoughts. What is required is genuine communication, not a heated battle of words. Beginning a response with a 'yes and' is a very good rhetorical technique, something that allows you effectively to deal with strong counter-arguments in an impressive manner. First of all you accept the objection by saying 'yes'. Then you offer your point of view, by saying 'and'. For example:

- 'Yes that is an important point you are addressing. And I would like to say the following on this point: ...'

- 'Yes, it is. And what you are saying leads precisely into what I would like now to discuss: ...'

- 'Yes, I'm glad you've raised that point, and I would like to come back to it in a moment. First I think it is necessary to talk about ...'

- 'Yes, thank you for raising this issue. And now that you have, I would like to offer an explanation along the following lines: ...'

- 'Yes, I'm glad you've voiced this matter. And in response I would suggest that what we are concerned with here ...'

If you use the words 'yes and' you are giving a positive and benevolent response to the opinion of another person whilst still holding the reins. 'Yes' is followed by your argument. Make sure you do not use the word 'but' after you have said 'yes'. Although 'but' sounds grammatically correct, it is unwise to say it from a psychological point of view. When we hear the word 'but' we expect that something negative is about to follow: 'You are a very good speaker, but ...' Now we can probably expect something that is going to contradict the first part of the sentence. An 'and' sounds much more neutral. All you are doing is linking a benevolent 'yes' with your opinion. 'Yes, you are a very good speaker and ...' The 'yes and' response helps you maintain your distance to the opinions of other people. So you are always in the position to react impressively and confidently without getting worked up or rashly belittling other people.

HOW NOT TO LOSE THE THREAD

You have prepared your speech or the contribution you wish to make to a discussion. This puts you in a superior position. Often the listeners are no match, on the spur of the moment, for your well thought-out arguments. For this reason they sometimes react in a slightly evasive manner. Your opponent counters with arguments that cannot really be considered counter-arguments. The danger lies in getting yourself so entangled in the inappropriate counter-arguments of your opponent that you lose the thread. Once you have been taken in by these inappropriate counter-arguments, it can be very difficult for you to return to your subject. Just how easy it is to get lost in the undergrowth of inappropriate counter-argument can be seen from the example of Veronica. She wants to leave work an hour early on Friday to go home. She has done several hours of overtime in the last few days because there have been so many customer orders. Now that everything has quietened down, she assumes that her colleague, with whom she shares her office, will be able to cope on his own on Friday afternoon. Her boss agrees on the basis that his two colleagues reach an agreement on who is going to stay until finishing time. Veronica has not prepared herself for any kind of argument. She assumes that her wish to leave early will be accepted by her colleague without any problems. But this is not the way it turns out. Veronica loses the thread of the discussion.

She says to her colleague: 'I'd like to leave early tomorrow. I really need to catch up on a few things I haven't had time to do this week because of all the overtime. It's okay with you isn't it, if I leave early?'

Her colleague's response is: 'Actually, I wouldn't be too happy about that. If the overtime is getting you down, I suggest you work more quickly in future!'

Whoops, Veronica had not reckoned with this kind of response. She is a reliable and fast worker. Nobody has ever accused her of being too slow.

Veronica responds with surprise and indignation: 'What? No one can accuse me of being lazy! What makes you think that? I actually sometimes miss my break when there's a lot to do.'

Her colleague: 'Yes, yes – but I have little sympathy for you when I see how much time you waste writing out invoices. You would save a lot of time if you worked with the client database. The reason we have it is precisely so that you don't have to keep on typing out all the client details whenever you write an invoice.'

Veronica is annoyed: 'But I do use the database! But for minor things. It's often just quicker to type an address.'

The colleague: 'You know, you waste a lot of time on these supposed minor details. One thing leads to another. In that respect you really are a time-waster.'

Veronica is now furious. She replies: 'I've been working here for five years and I do what I can. Nobody has ever complained about the way I work. You've only been here a year. But you've always got something to complain about.'

Now the colleague is also angry: 'That stupid mentality of "that's the way it's always been done". It's so irritating. Nobody listens to any of the suggestions I make about improvements.'

You have probably already noticed: this conversation is a typical example of how an argument can become confused. Veronica wanted to leave an hour early. That was her original aim. And where has she ended up? Having an angry conversation about the client database and time-wasting. How could this happen to her? The cause can be traced back to the beginning of the conversation. She clearly stated what she wanted. And then her colleague argued that he would have no objection to Veronica's going home early if she worked more quickly. Veronica got involved in this counter-argument. Instead of sticking to her initial aim she gave a response to the colleague's opinion. By doing so she lost her way. And every sentence took her further away from her goal.

Sometimes there are counter-arguments in which it is better simply not to get involved. All counter-arguments that widely digress from what you want lead you astray. In principle there is nothing wrong with talking about time-wasting, ways of working and the client database, but all in good time. In every discussion, every deal, it is important to stick to the subject. And this is in your hands. You cannot prevent your opponent from digressing. But you can determine whether you are willing to be drawn in. The art lies in immediately identifying digressions and secondary areas of conflict and getting straight back to the actual matter in question.

Women in particular are very good at being responsive towards the people that they are talking to, but it is precisely this positive ability that is their undoing. There are situations when it is important that we are not responsive. We need two important skills. Firstly: to be able to keep our sights on our goal. Secondly: to react slowly and prudently. Don't respond like a bullet from a gun. The quicker you respond the more likely it is that you will bark up the wrong tree. You need to maintain your distance from what is happening. Make sure you are slow to react. After the person you are dealing with has given his or her opinion, your most important consideration is: if I respond to this opinion, where will it lead me? If it distracts you from your goal, then use the 'yes and' response in order not to lose the thread. Veronica's conversation with her colleague would probably have taken a completely different turn if she had used the 'yes and' response.

Veronica: 'I'd like to leave early tomorrow. I really need to catch up on a few things I haven't had time to do this week because of all the overtime. It's okay with you isn't it, if I leave early?'

Her colleague's response is: 'Actually, I wouldn't be too happy about that. If the overtime is getting you down, I suggest you work more quickly in future!'

Veronica considers this for a moment and then says: 'We can talk about that another time. I think you can manage without me on Friday afternoon. I'm going to leave around two o'clock.'

Let us assume that her colleague still sticks to his counter-argument and still insists that Veronica could work more quickly. Veronica can still keep hold of the thread.

The colleague says to Veronica: 'But you could still hurry up a little. You don't use our client database enough when you write invoices.'

Veronica could reply: 'I'll think about it. And I'll put everything that needs doing this afternoon on your desk. There probably won't be very much.'

In order not to lose the thread, you must not attack the person you are dealing with because of their different opinion. Let them say what they have to say and assume your right to stick to what you want. The 'yes and' method prevents you from getting entangled in a pointless argument, in which nobody will escape unscathed, for the most part without any satisfactory result. There is nothing wrong in arguing with other people if you want to. To put it more clearly, if this argument leads to you achieving your goal, then let yourself be drawn in. If, however, like Veronica you want to finish work early, or have other plans, then make sure your conversation does not digress. Even if you have been drawn into the counter-opinion of another person and suddenly realise that you have digressed from your goal, you can still steer the conversation. Think things over for a moment and then offer up a 'yes and', bringing your concerns to the fore again. Every time you get angry during a discussion or conversation it may be a sign that you have got too involved with somebody else's opinion. Check what it is that you are talking about and whether it is relevant to your original goal. If it is not, then change the direction of the conversation without offering any great justification.

To conclude, one further note: do not turn your ability to convince people into a must, do not turn this into a new inner rule. You can win people over, but you do not have to do it at all costs. You can also let yourself be convinced by others. New ideas and creative solutions often only occur when all the people involved are prepared to loosen their grip on their own opinions and views or to let go of them completely.

Concluding Remark

We hope that with the help of our book you will be able to overcome the fear of speaking. We would like you to try out the exercises, techniques and tips and form your own experiences with them. Find out what works for you in the particular situations in which you are required to speak.

Perhaps you will find that you experience what many of our seminar participants did, that you have a unique and individual way of talking and that there is nothing wrong with this. And this unique, personal way of speaking will come to the fore if you take off the strait-jacket of inner rules. You then have your own, unmistakable way of speaking that you can build on and develop. We hope you have fun.

Index

Index compiled by Sue Carlton